TRICKS
OF
FATE

Escape, Survival and Rescue
1939-1945

TRICKS
OF
FATE

ESCAPE, SURVIVAL AND RESCUE
1939-1945

Morris Gruda

Edited and Translated from Yiddish
by Adam Fuerstenberg

mosaic press

Library and Archives Canada Cataloguing in Publication

Gruda, Morris, 1919-
        Tricks of fate : escape, survival and rescue, 1939-1945 / Morris
Gruda ; translator, Adam Fuerstenberg.

Translated from the Yiddish.
ISBN 0-88962-862-9

        1. Gruda, Morris, 1919-. 2. Holocaust, Jewish (1939-1945)--
Poland--Personal narratives. 3. Refugees, Jewish--Poland--Biography.
4. Refugees, Jewish--Soviet Union--Biography. I. Fuerstenberg, Adam,
1942-
II. Title.

D811.5.G778 2006   940.53'18'092   C2006-901180-X

Published by Mosaic Press, offices and warehouse at 1252 Speers Rd.,
units 1 & 2, Oakville, On L6L 5N9, Canada and Mosaic Press, PMB
145, 4500 Witmer Industrial Estates, Niagara Falls, NY, 14305-1386,
U.S.A.
info@mosaic-press.com

Copyright © Morris Gruda, 2006
Printed and Bound in Canada
ISBN 0-88962-862-9
Co-published by Mosaic Press and
The Holocaust Centre of Toronto, UJA Federation

Mosaic Press in Canada:
1252 Speers Road, Units 1 & 2,
Oakville, Ontario
L6L 5N9
Phone/Fax: 905-825-2130
info@mosaic-press.com
http://www.mosaic-press.com

Mosaic Press in U.S.A.:
4500 Witmer Industrial Estates
PMB 145, Niagara Falls, NY
14305-1386
Phone/Fax: 1-800-387-8992
info@mosaic-press.com
http://www.mosaic-press.com

www.mosaic-press.com

THIS IS THE THIRD VOLUME
IN THE HOLOCAUST MEMOIRS SERIES
CO-PUBLSHED BY
THE HOLOCAUST CENTRE OF TORONTO,
UJA FEDERATION

&
MOSAIC PRESS, PUBLISHERS

TABLE OF CONTENTS

Dedication
Acknowledgements
Preface
Foreword
Introduction

continued over

Dedication

I dedicate this book to the memory of my wife Malka (Manya) z"l who passed away on Feb 18, 2006 just weeks before this book was published. She was my true life companion and constant support during the fifty-nine years of our marriage. She was a shining star to all who knew her.

Your words and your sounds
Were captured by waves
And were delivered
To those who needed comfort.

You consoled everyone
To lighten their spirit,
Did you spare something
for your own consolation?

Morris Gruda

Acknowledgements

I have finally arrived at the moment I have been waiting for four years: the completion of my book describing my childhood in Poland, my survival during the Holocaust, my war-time survival in Stalin's Russia, and my fortunate immigration to Canada. I want to express my gratitude to my daughter-in-law Lena and my son Michael and their children in Jerusalem, my daughter Annette and her husband Leslie and their children in Toronto, who all inspired me to write my often painful memories. I have tried to stay true to the facts, to write in a simple, unexaggerated manner, and to control the of ten tragic emotions that I experienced during my effort trying to recollect the horrors I lived through.

I want to thank most of all my life partner, my dear wife Mania, for her support and for patiently enduring many hours of neglect while I struggled with these memories.

I take satisfaction in the fact that our children, and especially our grandchildren, will be able to read about and know their grandfather's childhood, and how a small segment of our family survived the greatest tragedy that our people experienced in modern times.

I also want to thank Professor Adam Fuerstenberg for translating and editing my Yiddish text. He tried to ensure that the translation fully mirrored the tone and rhythms of the original. It was a fruitful collaboration and understanding between us and for this I express my deep appreciation and gratitude. Because he, too, survived the Holocaust as a child in Russia, Professor Fuerstenberg could fully emphathise with the experiences I chronicled and this is reflected in the authenticity of the English text.

Finally, I hope this book will inspire others to realize that hardships in life do not have to be hopeless; one must not give in to despair but rather "Never Lose Hope."

Morris Gruda
October, 2005

Preface

I began my autobiography on October 31, 2001. Earlier that day I had received an e-mail from Lena, my daughter-in-law in Jerusalem, in which she had informed me that our mutual friend, Ben Grosman, who also lives in Israel, had completed his autobiography and had given her a copy. She appealed to me to write down my story. I had been thinking about this possibility for many years, but somehow I wasn't able to find the willpower to begin such an undertaking. I knew that if I would have to go back to those horrendous times it would be very painful and emotional. Nevertheless, over the years I did have occasions to speak to different groups about some of my experiences and, painful as it was, I "survived" the telling.

Recently I, like other survivors, had become alarmed at the assertions of Holocaust deniers that there had been no Holocaust, that there had been no six million Jewish men, women, and children starved, tortured, and murdered in the most systematic and brutal manner that the world had ever experienced. It became important to me that my children and grandchildren hear the truth of what happened directly from me so that they would have a personal defence against these lies. I wanted them to learn how one must act under such terrifying conditions and not lose one's humanity, to have the strength to overcome and to continue living a normal and just life. Now, as I begin to write my story, I pray that I will have the strength to complete my task and that my memory shall serve me well.

Morris Gruda

Foreword

When a world turns mad, when families are destroyed, when Hell is created on earth, it takes a great deal of personal strength and belief to survive, to build and to recreate.

Moshe Gruda has seen the evil of evils in this world, has walked through the Valley of Death and yet retained his dignity, his convictions, and his commitment to family life, the Jewish people and the State of Israel.

He has not wavered for a moment and his testimony, as recorded in this book, will serve as a lesson for generations to come.

His resolve to rebuild his own family, to participate in the rebuilding of Jewish life and unabashedly defend Israel are all hallmarks of the man known as Moshe Gruda.

Dr. Frank Diamant,
Executive Vice-President,
B'nai Brith Canada

Introduction

In the horrible history of genocides none has had a broader impact, nor has garnered more examination, than the Holocaust.

There have been studies and histories of almost every aspect of Nazi rule and of their plan to annihilate all the Jews of Europe. The most powerful indictment of their nearly successful genocide of the Jews has been the stream of personal testimonies that Holocaust survivors have published. Since Eichmann's trial in 1960, which seemed to break some sort of emotional barrier that had prevented survivors from recounting their experiences under the Nazis, thousands upon thousands of Holocaust memoirs have appeared..

However, one area of Holocaust experience has been largely ignored. This is the story of the almost 300,000 Polish Jews who escaped into Russian-occupied Poland after September 1939. Although their suffering bears no comparison to the horrors inflicted on their brethren in the ghettos, concentration camps and Nazi death camps, their epic struggle to survive in an impoverished Russia fighting to confront the German onslaught of June, 1941 also bears telling. They too were victims of Hitler. Tens of thousands perished from hunger, deprivation, and backbreaking slave labour in the Soviet gulag. Tens of thousands were also killed fighting in Russian-directed partisan units and in the Red Army.

It is just such a personal odyssey that *Tricks of Faith* describes. Morris (Moishe) Gruda, was only nineteen when his little shtetl Rozhan, so typical of the hundreds of such Yiddish communities the Holocaust consumed, was occupied by the Germans on September 8, 1939.

Until that fateful day, though surrounded by anti-Semitic hostility, the Gruda family had lived a typical and reasonably comfortable life, earned with incredible industriousness by Morris' mother, who ran a prosperous, home-based bakery, and by his shoe-making father. Life was punctuated for Morris by successive and enjoyable Jewish and general schooling, athletic prowess, Jewish holidays, and life-cycle celebrations in an extended family of over sixty grandparents, uncles, aunts and cousins. By the summer of 1939 Morris had already served two apprentice-ships as a ladies tailor and could look forward to success as a fine craftsman in a larger city.

All this changed with violent suddenness when the Nazis invaded. Within days, German carpet bombing created chaos all over Poland; refugees were forced to flee in all directions. Polish soldiers, especially Jews, shed their uniforms as the Polish war effort collapsed, and tried to meld into the general population. Among these Jewish soldiers fleeing the Polish military defeat were Morris' older brother Yitche Nussen and his brother-in-law Srulce.

The rest of the Gruda Family had escaped to Pultusk a few days before the Germans entered Rozhan; Pultusk was a larger town where Morris' pregnant sister – Srulce's wife – lived. Within days the German army entered Pultusk also. After a few days of terrorizing the local population, they brutally gathered thousands of Pultusk Jews in a large field and after robbing them of any valuables, drove them viciously east in the direction of the Narev River to what was expected to be the Russian side of occupied Poland. Convinced that they must get as far away from the conquering Germans as possible, young Morris led his little family group – his brother-in-law Srulce had hidden in an attic in Pultusk when the Jews were rounded up – on a harrowing four day journey through back roads and farmers' fields to the Russian side.

Luckily they were reunited with Srulce in Bialystok and, not being allowed to work there, they moved first to Pinsk, then to Sernik, a small town deeper in Russia. After more than a year in Sernik, where Morris was almost drafted into the Russian army but was rejected because he had come from German occupied Poland, he became convinced that the Germans would soon invade Russia and that the family must escape further east. Unfortunately, his father - tired of running away - refused to budge and so Morris, his older brother, and Srulce, decided to hop on one of the many freight trains heading east, hoping that once they were settled his father, mother, and two sisters would join them.

Eventually Morris was drafted into the Russian corps that built and maintained the railway lines required for the war effort, a backbreaking task which few survived because of the low status the service had and the inadequate rations provided. Morris, however, was very resourceful and convinced the commanding officer to let him find a sewing machine in the ruins of recaptured Stalingrad. Incredibly, he was able to find one and so was able to undertake additional, private tailoring work for the officer which brought him the means to buy food on the black market. This was a survival pattern in war-time Russia; there was never enough food from regular work and those who didn't manage some illegal income inevitably starved to death. Technically this turned everyone into a "criminal," but Morris never lost his moral compass and at crucial moments was even able to help others to survive.

There are heartwrenching episodes in the book. Even today the author can't forgive himself for not persuading his father to join the three younger men. As a result the more vulnerable members of the family were separated from their more vigorous men. The tragic consequence was that Morris' mother and two of his sisters – one the mother of his little niece – perished from hunger and disease. By pure chance, and in the nick of time, he was able to locate his surviving father, younger sister, and the little daughter of one of the sisters who died. Through Herculean efforts Morris was able to rescue them and to reunite what was left of the family, especially Srulce and his young child.

Morris Gruda's story of survival, while vividly unique and occasionally almost miraculous, is representative of the experience of Polish Jews "marooned" in the Soviet dictatorship during W.W.II. Many did not make it back. The author's special qualities, his resourcefulness, resilience, and amazing adaptability, and his single-minded determination to rescue his family, all contributed to his survival and his ability to return to a devastated Poland. After learning the horrible fate suffered by the rest of his extended family and experiencing the residual anti-Semitism still lingering in his birthplace, he realized there could be no Jewish life for him in Poland. With the assistance of the "Bricha," the Jewish Agency's illegal immigration apparatus in post-war Europe, he and his family made it to a Displaced Persons camp in occupied West Germany, where he married his life partner, Mania, with whom he eventually immigrated to Canada.

A successful businessman and philanthropist in Toronto,

and a noted Yiddish poet and writer, Morris is most proud of being a father of two and a grandfather of thirteen.

Adam Fuerstenberg
Professor Emeritus, Ryerson University

CHAPTER 1

Rozhan

I was born on October 14, 1919, in Rozhan, a small town about 80 kilometres northeast of Warsaw. It was a typical shtetl in Poland with about four thousand Jews living in close proximity to an almost equal number of Poles. I remember that I had already attended "cheder" (traditional elementary religious school) for a year when I was proudly able to write my birthdate on my fourth birthday. At three, my father had covered me with his "talith" (a striped tasselled prayer shawl) and carried me to my first "melamed," or teacher. He was known as Perchl, not a very nice nickname because it suggested a disease which testified to the severity of his teaching methods. I do not recall suffering with this teacher, but my parents must have been apprehensive because they took me out after only a month or six weeks and placed me with Reb Yitzhok - nick-named affectionately "der alter Yitzhok" - a short old man with a long white beard. He must have been a very kind teacher because I loved attending his "cheder." I was still so small that I had to stand on a little stool to be able to learn and read the "aleph- bet" (Hebrew alphabet). When the Rebbe pointed to an "aleph" and I repeated it successfully, a candy would suddenly fall from above. One time, when my father was standing behind me, I asked him where the candy came from. He explained that an angel throws down candies for little Jewish boys who learn their "aleph-bet" and "Torah" well.

We were seven in my family. My parents, Avraham Eliezer and Chana Mindl, my two sisters, Ruchl Gitel and Liba, ten and eight years older than I, and my brothers Yitzhok Nathan (Yitche Nussen) and Shloime Meyer, six and four years older than I. When I was five, our family increased by the arrival of my youngest sister Esther, born in 1925. We lived in our own two story house which had my parents' grocery store and bakery in the front and bedrooms in the back and upstairs.My father was actually a shoemaker, but when I was born he was helping my mother in the store. Some years later, he returned to shoemaking because my parents lost the store due to severe economic conditions.

When I was six and a half I began Polish public school. The school day was from 8 am to 1 pm. When school ended I would go home to get a bite from my mother, then I would rush to "cheder" which lasted three hours, ending just in time to hurry home for supper. Most of the children in the public school were Jewish, perhaps as many as two thirds, and there were a number of Jewish teachers. I actually loved school, not least because of my first teacher, Miss Zemmel, whom I adored. I also liked the principal, Mr. Ring, a very strict but fair man whom everyone respected.

In 1926 a momentous event occurred in our town. Electricity arrived! Of course, in our family we had to wait a few years longer; it was probably too expensive for us. Another event that year stands out dramatically in my memory. The great Alexandrer Rebbe, Reb Yitshok Menachem Mendl Danziger, was visiting his "Chassidim" (followers in a religious movement founded by an 18th Century charismatic teacher, the Baal Shem Tov) in Rozhan and my father, who may have been an "Alexandrer Chassid" at that time, took me to meet the great man.

When I was brought to him, he put both his hands on my bent head and pronounced a blessing over me. To this day I remember catching a sideways glance at my father's face shining with a satisfied, happy smile.

Other memories crowd in with this one. On the Sabbath, probably between the "Mincha" (early afternoon) and "Maariv" (evening) prayers, I remember my father and two older brothers in "shul"(prayer-house), while my older sisters were playing with friends; I was in the Sabbath-darkened house and I saw my mother sitting at the window for greater light and reading the "Tzena V'rena" (the women's stories of the Chumash rendered in Yiddish) with my baby sister in her lap.

At that time my brother Shloime and I attended a so- called progressive "cheder." A middle aged man and his son came from Makow Mazowiecki, a neighbouring town that served as the county seat, and they had opened a modern "cheder," despite the opposition of the (Melamdim) establishment. We were very happy because there was also singing of Hebrew and Yiddish songs in this "cheder", and teaching of "Tanach" (Old Testament).

This idyllic situation came to a sudden end when, in the summer of 1928, my parents had to sell the house to pay off all their debts. One day, a large, covered wagon with two enormous horses arrived. All our furniture and possessions were loaded onto it, then the family clambered on and we left for the larger town of Lomza, some fifty kilometres away on the road to the city of Bialystok.

The memory of this day is made even more poignant to me because among the friends and neighbours who came to bid us goodbye was Miss Zemmel. She looked upset that I was leaving, but when she asked me to give her a goodbye kiss I was so shy that

I went behind my mother's back and no amount of urging from the others was able to overcome my shyness. Later on I regretted that I had been so shy and didn't say goodbye to her. This regret became even more poignant spending a winter in Miami Beach, I met a man from my hometown and while we reminisced about our early schooldays I mentioned that I still remembered affectionally our first school teacher Miss Zemmel. Imagine my consternation when he told me that she had lived in Miami Beach until passing away only a few months earlier. And I had not even realized that she was Jewish! How much I would have given to have seen her again and to beg her forgiveness for my stubbornness seventy years earlier..

CHAPTER 2

Lomza

We travelled all night to Lomza, a much larger town with more than 30,000 people and a sizeable Jewish community. After a few hours, I fell into uncomfortable, restless sleep on top of the bundled up bedding. Although I was only nine years old, I already felt the drastic change in our fortune. I woke early in the morning just as we arrived at our apartment which my father had arranged a few weeks earlier. Half asleep, I still noticed that we had stopped in front of a tower-like structure in which there was a wide gate to enter a courtyard surrounded by two story connected buildings. We were able to reach our own apartment on the second floor through an entrance at the gate. We unloaded the wagon without going into the courtyard. What a contrast to our spacious, comfortable home in Rozhan! The apartment was one large room and a kitchen. Eventually we divided the large room into two parts, with all the children sleeping in one, and our parents and my youngest sister sleeping in the other. Life in Lomza was extremely hard.

Shortly after we arrived, the worldwide Great Depression arrived in Poland. My father was not able to find work as a shoemaker, so my mother tried to get some merchandise on consignment, things like socks, women's kerchiefs, blouses, undergarments, and so forth. Three times a week she would travel on market days to nearby small towns such as Kolno, Jedwabne, and Nowogrudek, to set up a little stall and sell her merchandise to the peasants. She would leave the house at three in the morning with a drover and his wagon - he usually had a number of such passengers - to arrive at the town at seven in the morning when the peasants arrived to sell their produce. She didn't come home till after nine o'clock at night. It was a very hard life for my mother, even though my older sisters helped out at home while she was away. In spite of her valiant efforts, there were days when there wasn't enough food for the family. I was already nine and attending the Talmud Torah on Sanatorska street, opposite the famous Lomzer Yeshiva.

My older brother Shloime was fourteen and had a beautiful mezzo-soprano voice. He soon became a member of the choir in the great synagogue, and shortly after, the soloist. I too, was accepted into the choir later, probably as much because of his influence as my own singing talents. As members of the choir we received a small payment, which we promptly turned over to mother, and our family had free tickets for the High Holidays.

Going to the rehearsals was a pleasure and we could also forget our hunger for a short while. When the"Yom Tovim" came and my brother sang solo I could see the pleasure and "nachas" on my parent's glowing faces. My older sisters didn't attend school at the time when I attended school, but they must have learned years before, because they read books in Polish and Yiddish. Our choir income was also supplemented by what my older sisters were able to earn as candy wrappers for one of the city's candy factories. Every few days the factory would drop off fresh candies and wrappers and pick up the wrapped candies that were ready. My brothers and I would help our sisters when we had a little extra time. Things were so desperate, nevertheless, that my father would occasionally go to the office of the Bund, which distributed food to the needy, and when lucky, he would return with a bag of flour or some other grain. As my father was strictly religious he didn't approve of the Marxist, secular Bund, but circumstances forced him to set aside his disapproval.

I was attending the fifth grade in the Talmud-Torah and doing so well that soon neighbourhood women approoched me to write their letters to relatives or husbands in the United States.

The content and main theme of the letters were almost always the same: a plea for assistance in their dire plight. I particularly remember one woman whom we called "di hoiche Bina" (the tall Bina) because she was extremely tall. Writing a letter for her meant at least three hours of work because she let loose a torrent of disjointed, whining complaints and requests for help. It was my job to put all this into coherent shape and provide some sense and progression in the letter. By the end of our session I was completely exhausted. The women would pay my mother something for my efforts, and Tall Bina never failed to come to our apartment to bring some money after she received help from abroad.

Our apartment was in one of the buildings owned by a man named Kulkin, and because the buidings surrounded a courtyard, the whole complex was known as Kulkin's Courtyard. The name of our street was Kshive Kolo, a street whose name can be translated as "crooked wheel". There were many tenants in this complex, but one especially drew my boyish attention. He was a milkman living on our floor, and he bought milk from farms in nearby villages and resold it to stores in Lomza. What attracted me was the fact that he had a horse for the wagon he used. It was an ordinary, white-grey draft horse, but to my boyish eyes it looked like a beautiful animal, fit for an ancient warrior or knight just like in the invented stories my imaginative oldest sister, Rochl Gitel, used to tell me. He would leave very early in the morning so as to be back in time to deliver his milk to the stores before the ladies arrived to do their morning shopping. Once he was finished, he would unharness his horse in the courtyard (our complex was located on the edge of the city) and take it out of the city to a grassy field (likely belonging to the city) to let the horse graze. To make sure it didn't run away he would hobble it by tying its two front feet very loosely so that it could move but not run. At around four or five in the afternoon he would return and bring his horse back to Kulkin's Courtyard where he had a stall for it. By the time he was ready to return to take the horse from pasture, I was already back from school and would eagerly watch for him.

He would ask me if I would like to accompany him and the horse to the field. He had no children so I, being the youngest on our floor, got his friendly attention. One day, when he was about ready to return to fetch his horse he asked me if I would like to come. Of course, I jumped at the opportunity, attracted by the chance to see the horse and also by the possibility of being out in the fresh air in the open field, a great contrast with our crowded tenement. On the way to the pasture he happened to mention that his horse was extremely afraid of a whip, so he never used one.

When he had untied the horse, he asked if I would like to ride it home. He picked me up so that I could get on the horse and I rode it bareback while holding on to the hair of its mane, as it had no saddle or harness.

At first the horse walked at a normal pace with its owner walking behind. After a little distance on the road, we suddenly encountered a group of Polish teenagers returning from fishing at a nearby river. Recognizing that we were Jewish, they began waving their long fishing rods and even managed to strike the back legs of the horse. In panic, the horse took off like a rocket with me hanging on to the horse's mane for dear life. In full gallop it covered the three kilometres to its stall in about ten minutes. For me, only ten years old and terrified, and unprepared for such a ride, it seemed like a lifetime. When the horse finally stopped, I was stiffly glued to the horse and could barely descent. Slowly I slid down, but I was so sore that I could hardly stand and, in my hands, I had two fistfuls of grey-like white hair from its mane. I could hardly walk up to our apartment, and when my mother saw how white with fear my face was, she asked in alarm where I had been and what had happened. I wanted to answer, but I was still so frightened that I couldn't regain my voice to tell her. I wasn't able to utter a word for almost half an hour. Ironically, this was a foreshadowing of a dramatic experience with a horse that I would have again, but ten years later, during the war.

At the Talmud Torah I attended, I still had little knowledge or awareness of secular subjects like math, geography, history, or Polish language and literature. Most of the curriculum was "Chumash", "Tanach", little "Gemarah", and even less Hebrew. Life was extremely difficult for us in Lomza; for almost four years my parents struggled to maintain the family and it was a miracle that they were able to send me to the Talmud Torah. My older brothers were already apprentices, Yitzhak Nussen to a cap maker and Shloime to a tailor. Of course, they didn't get any pay, so they couldn't help, but they were at least fed by their masters.

When I wrote the letters for the women in our neighbourhood, I also wrote to our family in the United States for help. That's how I first found out that my mother's whole immediate nuclear family was in America. I thought of America as a fabulous place; after all, every now and then we would receive money from there. How come, I asked my mother, we were not with them? My mother told me the following details. When her mother died and she was a small child of three or four- she could hardly recall her mother- her father, my grandfather Hertzko Gallant, remarried a young woman, Chana Liba, a lovely and able woman who was industrious and helped my grandfather to maintain the growing family which also included my mother's older sister, Bayla, and the two children born to Chana Liba and my grandfather, my uncle Mendl (Max) and my auntie Rivka (Beka). During the difficult years at the turn of the century my grandfather decided to go to the United States in the hope of finding work as a baker. He probably left in 1903 or 1904, and by 1908 he was able to send for his wife and two younger children, and we later learned that they also had a boy in the United States, my uncle Chaim (Haimie). He did not have enough money to bring his two older daughters because they were both already married and my aunt had a daughter, my cousin Lena.

In 1910 my grandfather arranged to have my mother and her sister and their families come to America. My aunt Bayla and her family left to join him in Newark, New Jersey. Tragically, we didn't. My father had some trouble with his eyes and the only Jewish doctor in Rozhan, or "felsher" (a sort of male half doctor or nurse), told him that he probably suffered from trachoma. He never attempted to go to another town for a second opinion and he now was afraid that he would be refused his papers during the medical examination at the United States Consulate, which one had to undergo before being allowed to depart for the U. S.

Ironically, as time eventually demonstrated, he likely had an eye infection which he neglected, because nothing happened to his eyes and he was able to work for decades after. My mother often pointed out that through my father's negligence and apprehension we were prevented from going to America. Had we successfully emigrated we would have avoided so much tragedy and suffering, to say nothing of the loss of my dear mother, my two sisters, and my oldest brother and their families during the Holocaust!

During the Great Depression I wrote a number of letters to my grandfather and aunts but we did not receive any responses. We were desperate and I wanted to know what had happened. As a boy interested in everything, I had at the time come into possession of a silly little book in Yiddish about witchcraft. Out of foolish curiosity I decided to follow some steps which the book outlined in order to trace someone who had vanished mysteriously. I don't remember all the steps, but on different pages it told me to follow instructions and included a procedure of timing, incantations, and some machinations witch included taking a sieve into which you had to insert a scissor. Imagine my shock when, at the end of the procedure, I ended up with a statement that said "the individual you are seeking is dead."Of course, I didn't tell my mother what I had done and I would by now have forgotten about the story except for a strange coincidence. Almost twenty years later, after I had arrived in Toronto as a Holocaust refugee, my American uncles and aunts came to meet me and to assure themselves that I was indeed their nephew. It was only then that I found out for the first time the reason we heard nothing from my grandfather. He had, in fact passed away in 1925, some six years before my experiment with witchcraft. My uncles and aunts explained that they had deliberately not written to us about his passing even when they sent us money. They had arrived as small children in U.S. and never learned to write Yiddish and, as well, didn't want to upset my mother and perhaps destroy her hopes of her father bringing her to America!

The closest relatives we had in Poland were my father's family. His father Shloime Meier Gruda had passed away when my father was still a young boy. My grandma Yenta Tzivia, his mother, and his two brothers and three sisters now lived in Rozhan or a nearby town. My oldest aunt Yitta Malka, her husband, Chaim Senderovich, and my father's brother, Moishe Hersh with his wife Genendl, lived in Rozhan. The other brother, Haskell and his wife, as well as my father's other two sisters, Bayla Lea and her husband Zailig and Esther Chana and her husband Sender, lived in the nearby city Makov-Mazowietski.

My grandma lived with my aunt Esther Chana, the youngest. I imagine that she lived with her because Esther Chana was
more prosperous than her sisters and brothers. Her husband was
a successful wagon manufacturer. Each of the brothers and sisters
had at least six children; we were 39 grandchildren, and there were
now also two great-grandchildren. When my grandmother came
to visit Rozhan, she always stayed with us. I adored her and had a
special relationship with her. For years I jealously couldn't accept
that she was also the grandmother of my numerous cousins. She
was always dressed meticulously, with flower-designed pleated
skirts, a caftan, beaded necklaces, high boots, and a velvet little hat
fastened with pearl-topped hatpins. Although she was petite, she
carried herself with such grace that she seemed taller. She had a
dark complexion and although she was only about sixty years old,
her face already showed the lines that her difficult life raising six
children had produced.

By wartime, in 1939, we were a close family of fifty-six
souls. Only eleven survived the war.

All through those nearly four years in Lomza I was terribly unhappy, as were my sisters. We were so poor that I hardly
had a "Bar-Mitzvah". I remember getting an "Aliya" in a small
"shtibl" where there was barely more than a"minyan." That was

it; no "seuda" or party. I was a man, but a very disappointed boy. Almost everyday I begged my parents to return to Rozhan, which in my childish memory was like a paradise compared to our present situation. Apparently my parents had been thinking along the same lines and so one day they decided to return. I know that I was very happy but for some reason I don't know why I have no memory of the actual move back, which could have been as vivid as the earlier exodus to Lomza.

We made it back to Rozhan in the Fall of 1932 and I can recall first living in one room in a basement in a two story building. Two small windows at sidewalk level looked out stingily onto the market, and we could see people's legs as they walked past our windows. Our condition was worse than in Lomza. Eight of us slept in a single room, a room which was bedroom, kitchen, living room, and workshop for my father's shoemaking. Added to this, the stone walls of the room were constantly damp. To this day I can't understand how we were able to endure it for the seven weeks that we occupied this room. During these weeks my father looked for work while my mother tried to sell at the market opposite the basement room the same merchandise she had peddled in the towns near Lomza. During those six or seven weeks I did not attend any school. Eventually my parents found a bright, more spacious room on the second floor of a house. It was a great improvement on the basement, although the steps leading to the room were in a terrible condition. Nevertheless, it was a great improvement on the basement, and I returned to school, but not Jewish school. When my parents registered me I had no public schooling in Polish subjects at all and so they put me at first in grade three. After three months, I was moved to grade four and near the end of the year I was moved to grade five and became one of the best pupils with the highest marks.

I liked school very much and was especially good in math, geography, and art, which consisted mostly of drawing. At that time I made a drawing of a lion's head and, from clay, an old man and an old woman which was displayed in the principal's office. The principal, Mr. Ring, who I subsequently found out was Jewish and a leftist, allowed a Hebrew teacher to teach the Jewish pupils "Chumash"(the Old Testament), reading it in Hebrew but discussing it in Polish. I imagine this fulfilled the State requirement for religious instruction. Our teacher, Arieh Buchner, was a very intelligent and knowledgeable young man from an eminent local family. Although he was teaching us "Chumash", he was actually the leader of the "Hashomer Hatzair"(a Marxist Zionist youth movement) in our town.

In 1934 when I finished grade seven, we finally found a house which suited our requirements. There was a large kitchen with a very large room attached which we were able to divide into a few separate rooms. Most importantly, my parents were able to hire a tradesman to build us a special oven in the kitchen that made it possible for my parents to run a bakery. A small room was also reserved for my father's shoemaking and repair shop. From then on our livelihood improved radically. Everyone in the house was working. My mother attracted people to the bakery. Every day she baked dark bread (razowo), bagels, and for Shabbats, challahs and spongecakes. On Fridays before Shabbat, the local women would come with their "cholent" in earthenware pots to bake overnight in our big oven. My mother would seal the oven doors with clay so the heat wouldn't dissipate overnight. In the morning after prayers, the women would come to pick up their hot pots filled with the delicious meal for Shabbats. Seventy years later I can still smell the tantalizing smell from the twenty or so cholent pots. Since the pots were so similar, it would occasionally happen that the rich man's cholent- with plenty of succulent flanken and kishke- would end up in a poor man's house, even though each pot would have some identifying mark. A frantic search would ensue to rectify the inadvertent error, but it was not always successful.

My sisters also bought milk from nearby farms which we sold by the litre. Whatever was not sold was poured into special earthenware jugs and placed in the coldest part of the cellar. A few days later it would yield a layer of sour cream at the top which we removed and churned into butter and "maslanka" (butter-milk), a form of light sour cream. The yoghurt which was left gave us cottage cheese after the water was squeezed out through cotton bags. Even the water was sold to farmers who fed it to their pigs.

We soon had a lot of customers because everything was fresh and tasty. My older two brothers worked at their trade and my father at his. My job was to chop wood for the oven and to help wherever necessary. My sisters helped with the milk products and the bakery. We all worked hard, but we were not short of food or clothing anymore. We were, indeed, fortunate because at that time almost seventy percent of the Jewish population in Poland lived in dire poverty caused by the lingering depression and the boycott of Jewish businesses sanctioned by the Polish government. The Polish population was encouraged to buy only from other Poles. At this time I was a problem. My parents weren't sure what to do with me. One day, when I had finished grade seven, the principal had come to our house to urge my parents to let me continue into the next stage, gymnasium. Unfortunately, the school I would have to go to was in a neighbouring city, Ostrolenko, some 27 kilometres north of Rozhan. This was not practical. "Melamdim" (religious teachers) came suggesting that I be sent to a "yeshiva" (religious college), but I was not too keen on that. I was getting Hebrew lessons at home twice a week, but my parents felt all this was not leading anywhere. In my heart I felt that they were right; I saw that everyone in the family was contributing but I was not. So the question became what kind of trade should I learn. Fortunately, there was no shortage of tradesmen who were willing to teach me a trade. In our town there was a very good ladies' tailor, but it cost money to become his apprentice. However, he was willing to take me for free, but I was not quite ready to go. A number of dramatic experiences came to a head and led me to decide to accept this opportunity.

Although I didn't attend Polish school, I did have a tutor for Hebrew and Talmud for a few hours each day. This gave me plenty of time for my favourite activities - sports. I played ping-pong, soccer (we called it "fusball'), and I was a very skillful jumper, both in the high jump and the distance jump. There was no formal playing field in Rozhan, but there was a flat field on the outskirts of the town which was used once a month for animal sales: pigs, chickens and geese, oxen, cows and calves, and goats, but mostly horses for which the field was popularly known as the horse market. The rest of the month Jewish boys would indulge in various games and especially soccer. However, my enjoyment of this field was to lead me to a frightening experience in which I almost lost my life. It became a precursor of my experiences in the war.

One midweek day, four of my friends and I were playing soccer on the field when we suddenly became aware that three Polish boys were throwing stones at us. We noticed that they were our age, about 14, sitting on a fence which bordered one side of the field. We stopped playing and asked them to stop, but they laughed and continued. I turned to my friends and said: "they are only three guys, let's chase them away". My friends agreed and I rushed towards the Polish boys. As I reached them and began fighting with the biggest one, I noticed suddenly that I was alone; my friends had run off and I was one against three. Nevertheless, I was strong and agile and could acquit myself well. Sure enough, I landed a terrific blow at my opponent's nose; he fell and began to bleed profusely and I used this occasion to make a strategic retreat by walking purposefully in the direction of the Jewish part of the town. I didn't make too much of this incident because skirmishes of this nature were an almost daily occurrence. Unfortunately, the violent epilogue of this incident was to catch up with me almost a year later and it had an effect on my attitudes which has influenced me all my life.

There was another incident at that time that also left an indelible impression that was to haunt me until very recently. Our river Narev was a beautiful stream with sandy beaches where we would occasionally swim or simply loll around in the warm summer sun. One day returning from the beach I encountered a strangely dressed group of people; curious, coming closer, I realized that these were Romany (once derogatorily referred to as gypsies). As I drew nearer on my way home, an older woman from the group, dressed in a red and black skirt and blouse, with a colourful kerchief bound around her greying head, motioned for me to draw near. I was fascinated and obeyed. When I reached her, she said; "hey, young boy, I can tell you how long you will live." Of course, I was intrigued, but I hesitated for a moment and asked her " how much will it cost? I only have a five groshen coin on me," and I took it out from my pocket. She took it and proceeded to examine my right palm. After a minute she very slowly said: "you will live eighty-three years." At that time, not so long after my "Bar-Mitzvah," eighty-three years seemed like an eternity. During some of my most difficult moments during the war, this woman's prediction would return to me and I wasn't too certain that she was right.

Just a year ago, during my operation for colon cancer, when I had just turned eighty two, her dramatic prediction came back to me. I had never before shared this episode with anyone, but now that I am approaching my eighty- fourth birthday, I recall with amusement my personal encounter with the Romany people.

I also became a member of the "Hashomer Hatzair" that same year. My religious parents were not too happy, as the "Shomer" had a reputation for hostility to religion. However, in our town the "Shomer" was the largest and most successful Zionist organization.

I was also writing poetry at that time. Occasionally I read my poetry to my mother and I had great pleasure observing my mother's face while I read. I could see her pleasure and the "naches" she had listening to me. This memory reminds me of what a remarkable woman she was. One couldn't find a better description than King Solomon's famous song "A Woman of Valour." She was an outstanding woman with a logical mind. I marvel even today about what she was able to do. She had six children to bring up; she had to run a business in which she was the baker and the chief salesperson for all the products like the milk and butter and cheeses. She had to make certain that the raw materials like flour and milk were available in the proper amounts. I used to go with her to the farmers to buy the wheat which I then helped her carry to the miller, a Jew, to be milled into flour for the bakery. We also had to separate the chaff from the flour. She was also extremely kind and charitable and was respected in the town. Often when there was a need to raise money to help an unfortunate family, my mother would always be invited to join the committee because everyone knew that if my mother asked, few would refuse her. She was of medium height, with a lovely face, a fair complexion and blue eyes bordered by light brown hair. Even now my vocabulary is inadequate to describe my mother's outstanding virtues. She was a model of a Jewish mother. May her "Neshama" (soul) be "tachat kanfei ha shchina" (next to the divine presence).

CHAPTER 3

A Disappointment

One beautiful day I happened to meet a young man in his twenties sitting at the riverbank. He was a stranger, but being obviously Jewish, we soon struck up a conversation. He was visiting relatives in our town and when I happened to mention that I wrote poetry he became very interested and told me that in Warsaw where he lived he knew quite a few well-known writers. I recognized many of the names he mentioned because I had been reading their work recently. He asked me to bring my poetry the next time we met. I did and he read it with rapt attention. Once he had finished my manuscript, he said to me "you will not be able to achieve anything in this town." You should be in Warsaw; there you will achieve something. Come back with me and I will introduce you to established writers. Don't worry, you can stay with me." A day or two later he came to our house to speak to my parents. He praised my work and was able to convince my parents to let me go with him to Warsaw. Of course, I was eager to go, but as time would show, neither of us understood the impracticality of this venture. A few days later we left for Warsaw in a covered freight wagon drawn by two horses with a few other passengers sitting on benches up front, away from the freight. We left in the evening and took the whole night to arrive in Warsaw, about 88 kilometres. We arrived around seven or eight in the morning at a way- station in the city where drovers brought produce and freight from the provinces. The place was called in Yiddish "By The Iron Gate."

From there we boarded a streetcar to Praga, a suburb on the east side of the River Vistula, the river which divides Warsaw. When we came to the apartment where my friend lived I noted the extreme poverty and began to feel disappointed. A middle-aged woman greeted us at the door and it transpired that she was my friend's older sister and it was clear that she was not pleased at her brother's having brought a stranger into their crowded quarters, which consisted of just two small rooms. She called him into the second room while I waited and when he came out he told me that I could stay with him for a few days and, in the meantime, he would try to find me accommodation across the river in the Jewish section. After a meagre breakfast of a piece of dark bread and tea, without sugar, he told me we would go into the Jewish section of

Warsaw to meet a well-known writer whom he knew. He told me to take along my hand-written manuscript and leave my little flour bag with the few items of clothing that I had brought with me. We walked to the nearest main street and took a streetcar.

I remember my curiosity as we crossed the Vistula River over a large bridge. After about forty minutes we arrived at Nalewki Street and we descended. We walked a couple of blocks towards Zamenhoffa and a side street whose name I have forgotten. Soon we arrived at a large four story building where there was a gated entrance into an inner courtyard. Because it was daytime the gate was not locked and we let ourselves in and walked up one of the many stairwells to reach the writer's apartment. After a couple of flights, we arrived at the door to one of the apartments and my friend rang the bell. A man opened the door and greeted us with a surprised look. Recognizing my young friend, however, his surprise quickly turned to a warm greeting. He was a tall man with a heavy build, but no beard and without a hat or "yarmulke" (skullcap) on his head which told me that he was not "frum" (religious) and since my young friend had already hinted at his own social radicalism, I surmised that this writer was probably something of a radical also. I believe his name was Shulman and judging by his apartment he seemed to make a living from his writing. I was introduced to him and my friend explained why he had brought me and mentioned my admiration for the Yiddish writers I had been reading. Our host brightened up even more and invited us into a little room, not much more than a closet, which served as his book-lined study. He sat down at the only armchair next to a small desk while he invited us to share an upholstered bench facing him. My friend had been explaining that he had been very impressed with my writing and so had suggested that I must come to Warsaw to meet established writers. The man nodded and turning to me, said, "so let's see what you have to show me." Trembling I handed him my well-worn notebook. He took a few minutes to read some of my poems and then began asking me what I had been reading. When I told him he nodded his approval, and then said the following. "There is no doubt that you have talent. You must read more and continue to write. No one can teach how to write creatively; you have to find this out by yourself, but reading widely will greatly help you and as you practice your writing you will, I'm sure, find your own voice." Even though he was encouraging, something in his manner to my young friend suggested to me that he didn't quite approve why he had brought such a young boy to the big city. He probably thought it was too early for me. Naturally I was very happy to hear his opinion and to get this encouragement. After a few pleasantries, we said goodbye and took our leave.

After we had reached Zamenhof again we passed a little restaurant and my friend said, "I have to go take care of something nearby, so you can wait for me in this restaurant and I will be back in about one hour." I went in and sat down at one of the four or five small tables. It was now at least five hours since I had eaten and I suddenly realized that I was, indeed, very hungry. I noticed that the proprietor was also the "kellner" (waiter) and he called me over to the counter where he collected the orders. He asked me what I would like. I checked if I still had the few coins which my mother had slipped into my hand. Taking a ten groshen piece (ten Polish pennies) out of my pocket – I wanted to spend as little as possible - I asked the proprietor what I could purchase with it. "A Kaiser-zemle mit puter" (a vienna roll with butter), he replied; then having an inkling that I was a poor boy from the country, he asked, "wilst ti?" (do you want tea?). I was afraid to answer yes in case he would ask for payment, but he added, "un gelt." (without money). It sounded to me like either an offer or a question and I nodded to both. "Est nisht darfen batzoln far di ti" (you won't need to pay for the tea.). I ate and drank appreciatively, but even a good sized vienna roll is not a full lunch. Still, I felt a little better and after thanking and paying the kind proprietor, I walked out into the sunny day to wait for my companion. As I stood outside leaning against the wall next to the restaurant, I marvelled at the rush of people passing in both directions in front of me. All the faces were Jewish and vaguely familiar yet they were all strangers. I felt alone. Everyone seemed to be in a hurry to get somewhere, their faces determined and serious, almost driven. Suddenly, I got a queasy feeling in the pit of my stomach and it wasn't the unrelenting hunger. I felt that I had made a very bad mistake in coming to Warsaw. I suddenly realized that I was not yet fourteen and I began to feel smaller than my actual size. To be frank, I was afraid; I had lost whatever confidence my ambition to become a professional writer – spurred on in Rozhan by my friend's urging – had given me. Suddenly it all evaporated and I wanted to be home and as close to my mother as possible.

A little after the hour, just as he had promised, my companion reappeared. He told me that he was trying to find a permanent place for me, and in fact had met a friend from "Hashomer Hatzair" who might be able to help us. We would meet her the next day not far from here. I was beginning to have doubts but I didn't say anything. The next day, we met the girl on Zamenhof street, not far from where we got off the streetcar. She actually was a very attractive young woman and spoke to us in Polish. However, it turned out that she too did not have a permanent place for me. I realized that my friend had been very naïve; his idealism and his enthusiasm at finding a young boy with writing talent had led him to believe that there would be no problem placing me in Warsaw and that everyone would be as eager as he was to nurture my talent. I wanted to return home, but the wagon which had brought me came only twice a week and I had just missed its return the previous day. After a few more uncomfortable days at his sister's I got up enough courage to tell my friend that the best thing for me would be to return to Rozhan, to my parents. He didn't argue; he too now recognized that it had been an honest mistake to bring me to the big city.

So ended my writing career in Warsaw and two days later he met me at the Iron Tower where the wagon gathered up the few passenger going to Rozhan. It was late evening, the sun had set and the sky was beginning to turn to a bluish purple as darkness was about to fall. He had hurried from his work at a printing plant to bid me goodbye. I thanked him and somewhat sadly we shook hands with the promise that sometimes in the future we would see each other again. The trip back was uneventful, but of course it lacked the feeling of expectation which made the uncomfortable ride to Warsaw bearable and even exciting. Now, even though we were travelling the same road through the night, my thoughts were gloomy and I wondered what I would tell my parents. With the wagon wheels scraping the road in a repetitive crunching, and my thoughts of failure haunting me, I hardly slept. When I came home I was unable to explain what had happened; I couldn't face my failure and didn't want to elaborate on it. Fortunately, my parents had an inkling how I felt and were more worried about the impact of my disappointment on me than about the expense and energy I had wasted on the trip. Both were happy to see me back; clearly, they had been worried about me and now I was back. They probably guessed that I had learned an important lesson, one which eventually would have positive results.

CHAPTER 4

Learning A Trade

I had returned chastened but the whole episode had only lasted 10 days. The summer was still ahead of me and I soon took up the activities and sports I had enjoyed before leaving. For the moment I didn't have to worry about my future and what I was going to do with myself, although before my trip my parents had already convinced the leading ladies' tailor in town to take me on as an apprentice.

One of the activities which I now resumed was my attendance at the "Hashomer Hatzair". It so happened that just as I returned, the local 'ken" (group) was organizing a little fundraising effort in order to send one of the "kovshim" (the youngest group of boys and girls) to the regional summer camp, the "Moshava." We needed 20 zlotys, a significant sum considering that a worker in our town might earn around 10-12 zlotys a week. The local movement promised 10 zlotys, but we – the "kovshim" – had to raise the other ten. The "Shomer" owned the main library in town, very popular with the young people, and used heavily. I found out that they needed someone to help to rebind and restore the books which were falling apart from such frequent use. Soon I found myself helping to restore the books. The tools were very primitive, but the people who were doing it knew their job and taught me what to do. Within three weeks, working every evening, I had earned 5 zloty and through the efforts of the rest of my group we soon had the ten zlotys required. My counselor, the "madrich," (the leader) wanted me to go, but the movement's practice required that the whole "kvutza" had to vote by secret ballot to choose who would be the privileged one. I was lucky, or perhaps our "madrich" had done some lobbying on my behalf, and I was chosen to go to the "Moshava". Needless to say, I was very happy and proud, though I'm not so sure I can say the same thing for my parents. After all, the movement was not friendly to religion; attending a group meeting once a week was one thing, but going away to be under their influence for three weeks was quite another. Nevertheless, I got my way, and one fine Monday I found myself again on a cart drawn by a horse going in the direction of Chechanov, to a village called Golota, where the regional movement had rented a farm house next to a small river. Here they gathered boys and girls from the various little towns in the area.

The camp was a lot of fun and I met young people from other little towns in the entire region; but I also remember that there was not enough food and we were constantly hungry. We had many activities and a lot of wonderful singing but too little bread, the staple, usually covered with a tiny bit of jam. One day, while playing in the narrow and shallow little river that ran beside the farm, also called Golota, we found that it was full of little perch, hardly eight or ten inches long. We had nothing to catch them with, but I noticed that some of the fish swam up against the shallow banks of the river, in some places where the flow of the river had created little rills or mud tunnels.

I kneeled in the water alongside one of these little mud tunnels and stuck my two hands into the water at each end of the little tunnel. Sure enough, although most of the fish slipped through my eager hands, I was able to catch the occasional one. Full of joyous excitement, I threw the ones I caught as far up the bank as I could and soon the other boys brought a big pot and put them in. That evening at supper, although we didn't have a real cook, the councilors managed to fry the fish and we had the first delicious and satisfying meal we had had since arriving. When I returned home my mother remarked that I had lost a lot of weight, but rather than being alarmed, she smiled and said "dos lejb falt nisht wajt" (flesh doesn't fall far from the body). Then she set about to have me regain what I had lost. For the next two weeks I received double portions of everything, my mother's wonderful cooking and baking. I was no reluctant bride; I ate like a pig- if you will pardon such an unkosher analogy- and soon had regained my former weight and then some, since I was beginning my last significant growth spurt. Playing sports regularly, I had no trouble turning the calories to height and muscle and reached adolescence in a very healthy state.

This wonderful summer soon came to an end and after a few weeks it was time for me to report to the ladies tailor who had agreed to take me on as an apprentice. His name was Natan Schredny and his pretty wife was Zissl. They were a young couple who were only in their mid twenties and had been married for about four years. They had a beautiful little boy named Kuba, a diminutive of Jacob, and we became very attached. Soon he refused to take his afternoon nap unless I told him a story. I would take him into the main bedroom, put him in his crib and slowly got him to fall asleep as I told him a story. When he made a fuss, the mother would come into the large kitchen, which also served as the workroom, and would ask me, "Moishe, go tell Kuba a story." I would look towards the master and he would smile gently and nod that I should go ahead. I can never forget the beautiful smile that animated Kuba's face when I came over to his crib to begin telling him a story. He was exceptionally beautiful, with blond curls and bright blue eyes, angelic cheek and lips, looking like one of those cherubs who had just stepped out from a Renaissance painting. I came to love him very much; there was such trust in his face when he turned to me and I still feel his affection. Whenever I think of the million and a half children the Nazis murdered during the Holocaust, it is his sweet innocent face that I see and the pain becomes more intense!

I began my apprenticeship by learning to make sure that the irons used for pressing were constantly hot and available to iron the garment at each stage and then, again, when the garment was complete. After a few months of this work, my master began to teach me to sew. At first I learned to "fastrige" which involved temporary stitching every few centimetres to keep parts of the garment together until it was sewn properly. Once the real sewing proceeds, the "fastriges" are removed. Eventually I was given simple parts to sew and, as I made rapid progress, by the end of the second year I had become a 'gezeln," in other words, a journeyman who could expect to get paid a wage. However, during my two year apprenticeship I didn't neglect my thirst for knowledge. I read all of Mendele Mocher Sforim, Sholem Aleichem, and I.L.Peretz, and became immensely impressed with the richness of the Yiddish language and its literature, and I also read Yiddish translations of the Russian classics like Pushkin, Dostoyevsky, Tolstoy, Gorky, Chekhov and others. I even read Yiddish translations of French writers like De Maupassant and Jules Verne, as well as American writers like Jack London and Upton Sinclair. There was even a Yiddish translation of Knut Hamsun which I managed to devour. I was insatiable. I must say that the Russian authors appealed to me most. Nor did I neglect my athletic activities and played all kinds of sports.

One day my master sent me to the post office which was quite a way from the shop and almost on the other side of town, away from the Jewish area. After I completed my task at the post office, I began making my way back the same way I had come. A few hundred meters from the post office there was a public school where no Jews attended. As I neared the school I suddenly noticed a group of Polish boys, probably from the school, standing in the middle of the road where I would have to pass. Some of them were holding sticks in their hands. My awakening apprehension turned into outright fear when I recognized one of the boys as the fellow with whom I had the fight a year earlier on the soccer field. He had grown into a strapping youth. I knew I was in trouble and not knowing what to do I suddenly turned around and started running in the opposite direction which led to the outside of the town. This was a foolish and dangerous decision. I turned my head and I saw almost twenty of the boys chasing after me and in a few minutes I was already beyond the town. The town road stopped. I was now beyond the houses and open fields were rising towards hilly ground. I ran up the nearest hill and just beyond it was a drop towards a cobbled highway that led to Pultusk. I was breathing heavily and losing the race. Just as I began to run in panic down the hill towards the road, I stumbled over one of the rocks on the slope, fell and began rolling down to the edge of the road.

The Polish boys now caught up and descended on me like a pack of wolves, hitting me on the head and body with their sticks. They were so numerous that there was no way for me to protect myself or to fight back. Soon I was bleeding profusely. I had been hit on my face and I felt the blood in my mouth. I was still conscious though very weak and couldn't move a limb. Seeing this, a few boys retreated up the slope, while the rest stood around because just then a farmer with a wagon was approaching. Seeing the commotion, he stopped and demanded to know what they were doing. In his wagon he had a long tree that he had just trimmed;

his axe was still buried in the tree trunk. One of the bigger boys ran over to the tree and pulled the axe out; then he came over to me, raised the axe over my head and seemed about to strike me. I was so weak and defeated from the running and the blows that I was almost indifferent to what was about to happen. I just closed my eyes and waited for the inevitable. Suddenly the farmer said something with an authoritative voice and took the axe from the boy, then got on his wagon and drove off. The remaining boys talked among themselves for a minute and satisfied with their bloody work, then went up the hill to join their friends. For a while I still heard their voices on the hill, then there was quiet and I realized that they had miraculously left. After a while, to make sure they had really left, I tried to lift myself up. But I couldn't, I was still so weak. My body and head were hurting badly but I was alert. It was beginning to get dark and I tried to think what to do next. As I lay there helplessly, I suddenly noticed a horse-drawn carriage coming slowly up the hill from the same direction as the earlier wagon. When it was quite near me I raised my arm and gave a scream. The driver stopped and came down from his coachbox and approached me. In Polish he asked me who I was and I answered him in Yiddish because I had recognized him as a neighbour who lived a block from my parents' bakery. He lifted me up, helped me into the empty carriage, and drove me home to my parents.

It was dark when we arrived home. My mother ran out alarmed and bewildered as the driver helped me off the carriage. Soon she was washing the blood off my face and my other wounds as I told my parents what had happened to me. Needless to say, my parents, while disturbed to see me bleeding, were overjoyed to see that I was not seriously hurt. The next day my father and I went over to the city hall only a block from where we lived. It housed the small police station of our town. My father told the policemen who were there what had happened to me. One of them told us to come the next day and a policeman would go with me to the Polish school and I would point out the boys who had beaten me. When we came home and my father told some of our neighbours, they began to dissuade us from doing this. They reminded us that the police were as anti-Semitic as the general population and this action would create more problems than it would solve. Every week our Jewish community suffered attacks from the Poles, especially on Sundays when they would stream out of the church into the market where they would wreck the Jewish stores. On such days you could not find a single policemen; knowing what was going to happen, they would make themselves scarce. So my father decided to drop the whole thing. In such circumstances it was not advisable to look for justice from Poles. This was the end of my terrible

experience.

CHAPTER 5

The Clouds Begin to Darken

At home life was following in a normal pattern. We were all working except for my youngest sister, Esther, who was only nine, and we were prospering. As in every shtetl in Poland, life centered on the observance of Shabbat. All week we looked forward to Shabbes, with its holiness and festivity. By Wednesday we could already feel the impending holiday. On Thursday morning my mother would go to the butcher to buy "rinderns," beef for stewing, and later in the afternoon she would use the rolling pin to expand the egg dough that would become the egg noodles for the Friday night chicken soup. My oldest sister, Rochl Gitel, would then cut the stretched dough into fine "lokshen" (noodles) and tiny square "farfel." Challas, the braided egg bread for Shabbat, was no problem as we were baking the same thing for many of our customers along with the traditional sponge cake, "leykech." Gefilte fish were also part of the women's work on Friday, along with delicacies like "tzimes" (a carrot, plum, and sugar mix), potato "kugels", and "kishke" (derma stuffed with a mixture of flour, fried onions, and chicken fat – schmalz).

My main job on Friday morning, before I went to work, was to take the live chickens to the "shoichet," the ritual slaughterer, to have their throat cut and the blood removed. My mother and sisters would then pluck the chickens by hand, then singe them over a small fire to remove the last small feathers, and then render them kosher through salting and rinsing out any blood that might have remained. The last major task for the women was to prepare the "cholent," the delicious mixture of potatoes, barley, beans, and beef flanken and bones. Just before the arrival of Shabbat on Friday the huge earthenware pot with this mixture would be put in the baking oven to simmer overnight and provide a delicious hot dish for lunch the next day. Most families didn't have a baking oven like ours, so the women from the neighbourhood would bring their pots to simmer in our oven. This sometimes led to hilarious situations the next day because the pots were very much alike and the heat didn't allow for any identifying objects. The result was that some picked up the wrong chulent and then both parties would rush back to us to exchange. Of course, if you were poor, you could sometimes end up with a rich man's chulent and enjoy a special treat.

Two tranquil years passed. It wasn't that we were un-aware that Hitler had come to power in Germany and was begin-ning to make life very difficult for German Jews, but it all seemed quite far away. People in our town only began to follow inter-national events more closely with the outbreak of the Civil war in Spain. The Spanish Civil War loomed larger than it otherwise might have because many Jewish boys from Poland smuggled themselves into Spain to fight with the Spanish Republican forces. These young men had become radicalized by the social and eco-nomic conditions in Poland during the Depression and were part of the generation which distanced itself from its traditional reli-gious roots. Whether they were Zionist, Bundist, or Marxist, most were progressives and aware that this was a war between fascism and democracy. They were an idealistic generation and quite a few wanted to join the fight against Franco, seeing him correctly as a surrogate for Hitler's and Mussolini's fascism. Since I was in the Hashomer Hatzair, and always an avid reader, I was especially aware of these developments. My master at work was one of the few people who had a radio in our town. It was a rather primitive device which only one person could listen to at a time by wearing an earpiece. I was already sixteen, my Polish was very good, so my master asked me to listen to the main newscast and translate for him and other employees, and even for some people who came in from outside especially to hear the news. By then I had ceased being an apprentice and had become a "geseln," a journeyman, and earned money from my work. Of course, the money went directly to my mother, but when I needed something – a suit, a coat – I would go with my mother to buy the material and then we would settle on a particular tailor to do the job. At the end of 1937, my oldest sister Rochl Gitel married a man from nearby Pultusk, a larger city 28 kilometres northwest of Rozhan on the road to Warsaw. Her husband was a plasterer and was frequently employed and was prospering.

The wedding took place in our home with the chupah (wedding canopy) set up outside in the yard. There was no such thing as having a wedding in a synagogue or a rented hall. For weeks ahead our women, together with female relatives, friends, and neighbours began baking and making the dishes that didn't require refrigeration. The main food was prepared a day before the actual wedding, just as all the relatives from neighbouring towns began arriving, especially from Makow-Mazowiecki. With my grandmother having forty grandchildren, the total family, with in-laws, probably numbered close to eighty, a sizable crowd for a wedding in those days, especially in a small town. Out-of-towners slept over at relatives or generous friends.

The wedding was beautiful, what with the delicious food and treats, klezmer musicians, a"badchan" (a clown-comedian), and chassidik dancing, the men and women dancing separately. After "sheva broches"(the seven parties celebrating the seven blessings that conclude the festivities) at various relatives, the guests left and the bride and groom went to Pultusk where they made their home.

Early in 1938, I told my master in Rozhan that I was leaving for Pultusk. My new brother-in-law had found a position for me with the most famous ladies' tailor in Pultusk, Golomb. Leaving the Shrednys was not easy, especially parting with their little boy Kuba whom I had come to love like a little brother. But my master, though surprised that I had secured a position at such a prestigious tailor in Pultusk, understood that this was a great opportunity for me and wished me well. It was an especially fortunate move be-cause my new master gave me much more responsibility which allowed me to develop in my skills as a ladies' tailor. I roomed with my brother-in-law's elderly parents, right across the street from my sister, but ate my main meal in my new master's home. They were lovely people and treated me like one of their own fam-ily. They had four sons and one daughter; the oldest son had made "aliya" to Eretz Yisrael and the other four children worked with their father in the tailoring room in their spacious apartment. I was the only outside employee.

I felt very comfortable with this family and in addition I was very happy that they soon trusted me with complicated work. I was making excellent progress in my profession. In those days you had to be able to make a complete garment from start to finish. This entailed first taking a measure of the lady customer after she had decided with the tailor what kind and style of garment she wanted. A good ladies' tailor had to know designing, styling, and every part of creating a good garment. He had to advise the customer on what material best suited her and the style she had chosen. My master had a very good reputation in the city and in neighbouring communities.

I worked through the fall and all winter of 1938 and into the spring of 1939. I left for Pesach at home in Rozhan, but we agreed that I would return in August since summer was the slow season in tailoring. When I came home I immediately began to help prepare the bakery for baking matzos for Pesach. There was a lot of work. Weeks before Pesach we had to clean the house from the "chometz" (leavened food, since on Passover only unleavened food is permitted). We bought a wagon load of cut trees which I had to trim and chop into small sections to use in the oven. My mother then bought sacks of flour and we hired women to prepare the dough and then to knead it. Then it was rolled into thin, round shapes which were punctured with tiny holes to allow air during the baking process. We employed at least fifteen women for these tasks and my mother had the difficult work of skilfully flipping the malleable, thin, 15 inch diameter wafers into the oven without tearing or dropping them on the floor. There was no packaging. Families came and purchased kilos of baked matzos, wrapping them in laundered white sheets to make carefully sure that none broke on the way home. An average family would buy a "put," which was sixteen kilos, close to forty pounds; along with potatoes and eggs, it was the staple at a time when there were only a few dishes eaten, and a family with 3 or 4 or 7 children had to ensure that there was enough over the eight days of Pesach. The broken matzos were crunched into matzo meal which, turned into kneidlach or baked dishes, was another staple at every dinner. Nothing was wasted.

Although there was great poverty in Poland at this time, we were relatively well off. All of us were working and as we were in the food business we had plenty of food. We ate meat almost every day, an unheard of situation for most Jewish families. Also, since some of us worked in tailoring we were well dressed. In fact, the family managed to save money and we were able to provide my sister with a respectable dowry. We also had a "Jewish" animal in our house: a tomcat with sparking green-yellow eyes. I had raised him almost from birth. I loved him very much and he seemed to reciprocate. He was not only part of the family, but a very important part of the business. A bakery had to have an aggressive, clever cat and he was very clever indeed. For instance, when my mother would return from the butcher almost daily, he knew when she was almost a block away and had learned how to undo the latch on the front door from the inside. He would jump on it with all his weight and wait for my mother at the open door. As always, she gave him his portion of goodies before she even walked into the kitchen.

My oldest brother Itche Nussen was at that time in the Polish army, serving in the cavalry, the "Ulans" (this was the Polish idea of a mechanized army: horses!). Occasionally his unit would pass trough our town during maneuvers and we would stand on the shoulder of the road to see him in his beautiful green uniform, riding stiffly on his huge horse with a lance in his right hand, spurs on the back of his boots, and a long sword at his side. How proud I was to see him and, indeed, it was not usual for a Jewish boy to serve in the cavalry. He was a broud-shouldered, strapping young man, and because we were well-fed at home there was no way for him to avoid service, Many Jewish boys tried to avoid military service by starving themselves. Through the summer of 1939 I stayed at home, waiting for the working season to begin. It was an ideal summer. Although I had left the Shomer Hatzair because their political views were too Marxist for me, I still socialized with some of the "chevra" (group) I had belonged to. The Shomer Hatzair in our town was disintegrating because its guiding spirit, Arieh Buchner, had left for Palestine in 1937 and was followed by others from the older leadership group. So we younger "shomernicks" were left increasingly on our own. I paired off with a pretty, black haired girl with sparkling, merry dark eyes, lanky and almost as tall as I. Her name was Masha. Together with friends we would go to amateur plays or concerts, or walk in the nearby countryside. I was still involved with sports and I read whatever came into my reach.

Time passed rapidly. The political situation was charged with impending storms. We could feel a catastrophe approaching although we could not imagine its final dimension. The borders of Poland were becoming virtually sealed to emigration and the Polish population was becoming aggressively anti-Semitic. While they themselves were under threat from the Nazis, they couldn't avoid being influenced by virulent Nazi hatred of Jews. Rozhan was a

town in northeast Poland, about 90 kilometres from Warsaw. It
was strategically located on the western shore of the river Narev,
a tributary of the river Bug which in turn flowed into the Vistula.
Because the western side of the river is hilly, the town overlooks
all the eastern shore and this makes the town easy to defend from
the east. This gave it strategic importance during its more than
1300 years of history. The eastern shore was overgrown with dark
pine forests and, because there were no polluting industries, the
town attracted tourists who came to enjoy the clean air and the pic-
turesque landscape. A favourite tradition was to rent accommodation from the farmers in the small villages nearby, like Kashevitze
which could be seen from the tallest hill on the western shore.

Every Tuesday and Friday were market days when the surrounding farmers brought their produce for sale to the townspeo-
ple. Vegetables, grains, all kind of dairy products and fruit from
the abundant orchards, as well as a variety of fowl, every thing
that the rich surrounding earth produced, was displayed for sale.
The market was a huge square area in the middle of the town surrounded by small shops, most of which were owned by Jews who
supplied the peasants with all their needs. Once a month, on a
Tuesday, there would be an even more elaborate market with mer-
chants from surrounding cities bringing their wares for sale. There

were even some itenarant entertainers like jugglers and acrobats. In conjunction with the monthly market there would also be a livestock market on the field where we used to play sports. Finally, once a year the really big market would be held when tens of thousands would come from many towns to our city to trade. Usually a circus would also arrive, attracted by the tens of thousands of people drawn to the big annual fair. It would be set up right in the middle of the market square and it also attracted scads of thieves and pickpockets.

Summer brought another diversion with its "merry Sundays." This refers to the rafters, river-men who rafted huge logs from upriver to the river Bug and then the Vistula whereby they reached the Baltic at the ports of Gdynia and Danzig, to be shipped to customers the world over. These river men were a rough lot, illiterate, dirty ruffians. These river "rats" built themselves makeshift wooden shacks on top of the huge rafts of logs they were bringing downriver. On Sundays they would moor their rafts near the town, go to church in the morning, and then raise hell in the market square after filling themselves with cheap alcohol. Their favourite activity was to break into the surrounding Jewish stores, smash the windows, break anything else that wasn't nailed down and steal as much of the merchandise as they could reach. The five man police detachment in Rozhan would have had difficulty controlling these drunk ruffians. But they themselves were anti-Semitic and made sure to make themselves scarce on those days.

I had a lot of friends in town, Jewish of course, and two, Hershel Pien and Chaim Hersh Baylis, were especially close. We had a lot of adventures, dated together, and had a lot of fun. In this little Rozhan, with barely four thousand Jews, all the Jewish political factions in Poland were represented, from Mizrachi to the Bund. We also had followers of all the major Chassidic dynasties, as well as a number of self-help institutions like" Bikur Cholim" (looking after the sick) and "Gimilat Chesed" (an institution to loan money without charging interest). Since the town had no industries, there was a lot of poverty, but regardless, Jewish life was vibrant and full of activities. Of course, understandably, the youth of the town tried to leave. A few succeeded but the majority didn't until destruction came to all Polish Jewry and a thousand years of our history and culture vanished forever.

Our Rav was the religious head of our community. I remember him as a tall, distinguished man with a full round white beard. His sermons were difficult to follow because his diction was not clear. The learned men of the town said, however, that he was a great "Talmid-Chacham," a great Torah sage. He never walked by himself but was always accompanied by the "Shames", the synagogue beadle. He too was a tall man, but younger, with a thick black beard. He was nicknamed "Bechinom," which translates "for nothing." The Rav had seven daughters, all married to rabbis, but only the youngest lived in Rozhan. She had married only two years before the War, a young, very handsome rabbi. About six months after the wedding, the old Rav suddenly passed away from a stroke. All the son-in-laws and many other noted rabbis came to the funeral. The most notable was the rabbi of Radom, Rabbi Kestenberg, renowned in all of Poland.

It was assumed that the young son-in-law of the Rav would inherit the position of religious head of the community. The young Rabbi was very impressive in his own right. However, there are always people who don't accept the logical solution to anything and so there was some opposition. The funeral turned out to be very dramatic. All the eulogies from the rabbis, quoting all kinds of passages from the Torah, stressed support for the young Rabbi, but some members of the audience interrupted with shouts that they would not accept the new Rabbi. I will never forget the tension in the synagogue until Rabbi Kestenberg, the last speaker, stood up to deliver his eulogy. He was a powerful and dramatic speaker and soon had almost everyone in tears. As young as I was, his speech made a powerful impression on me as it did on everyone there. By the end of his speech the opposition had melted away and as the coffin with the dead Rav rested near the Bima, one could hear shouts of 'Mazal-Tov' to the young Rabbi on his succession. Thus was the new Rav proclaimed, but not for long!

A year later, in August of 1939, Russia signed the infamous treaty of non-aggression with its arch-enemy, fascist Germany. The situation had become desperate and a few days later, on Friday, September 1st our radio announced that Germany had invaded Poland along the entire border. There ensued chaos and total confusion among the Jews in our town. No one knew what to do. Nevertheless, I remember clearly that fifteen women still managed to bring their "chulents" for my mother to put into the oven so there would be Shabbat lunch after prayers.

CHAPTER 6

Escape from Rozhan

On the first Friday of the War it appeared that the whole world was engulfed in darkness. Jews instinctively felt that they would suffer more than any other people. Nations might have to surrender their independence and freedom, but they would survive and endure. Jews would pay with their lives; our history had taught us that. After a hasty Friday night meal, very unlike our festive ones introducing the Sabbath our family sat together to try and decide what to do. Should we run and leave our house and possessions? And where should we run? Everybody we knew who had decided was moving East, away from the on-coming German armies. We also felt that this was the right direction we had to take. However, my sister had moved to Poltusk, west of Rozhan, after she had married about a year earlier. Her husband had been called up and was in the army and she was six months pregnant with her first child. So we decided to join her in Pultusk. That same evening my older brother Shloime and I went down to the basement cellar under the kitchen, where we kept things that needed to be cool, and dug a large hole in the earthen floor. Then we buried the family's prized possessions; our sowing machine, the Shabbat candelabra, other valuables. Early next morning my father went out to some peasants he knew to hire a farmer with a horse and wagon. When he returned we packed our clothing, bedding, and as much food as we had in the house. By ten o'clock we were ready to go. I was sent ahead on the regular bus that was still running its route from Bialystock to Warsaw and made stops in Rozhan and Pultusk. We wanted our sister to know that we were coming. In fact, I arrived just after eleven, some three or four hours before the rest of the family.

Of course, my sister was very happy, if surprised, to see me, and overjoyed to hear that her mother and father and most of her family would soon arrive.

Early in the afternoon my parents with my two sisters and my brother Shloime arrived at my married sister's apartment in Pultusk. My brother and sisters had mostly walked the entire distance as there was not enough room on the small farming cart full of our household effects. Occasionally my father would let each of them take his place on the cart to regain their strength. We unloaded the cart and let the anxious farmer return home.

In Pultusk the situation was no better than in Rozhan. There was also chaos and panic; people didn't know what to do. Exhausted, we arranged ourselves in my sister's small apartment and after a quick supper dropped off into a fitful, disturbed sleep. The next day, Sunday, we found out from neighbours that the radio reported that England and France had declared war on Germany. For a moment we thought that there was hope, but it was only a declaration of war; there was no tangible consequence. In the meantime the German juggernaut rolled over Poland on all fronts and the "blitzkrieg" were closer and closer to us. We tried to buy food but almost all the stores were shut; even when something was available, no one wanted Polish money. People were in despair. The Polish Foreign Minister, Colonel Beck, continued to declare on the radio that Poland wouldn't yield to the German enemy. During the few days we spent in Pultusk we heard fantastic rumours: that England and France would soon halt the German advance. Naturally these were empty rumours, but people wanted to be encouraged. Soon we were hearing that, in fact, the Germans were approaching Pultusk.

By Tuesday afternoon, the fifth of September, we could distinctly hear artillery cannonades on the northern outskirts of the town. We sat silently listening to the bombardment in the distance.

Suddenly, at eight o'clock, my brother-in-law Srulche burst in. He had been stationed with his unit in the town and decided to run home in full gear from the shattered Polish garrison stationed on the outskirts of the city. He told us that the German artillery was bombarding the military barracks and there was no military resistance at all. All the senior officers had disappeared; the enlisted men also scattered. Now the bombardment was distinctly closer. Along with other neighbours we decided to go down to the cellar of the apartment building and there we sat in the dark, fearful like rats, waiting for the bombardment to stop. Around midnight it ceased and a deathly silence descended on the town. After a little while we decided to return to my sister's apartment, but no one slept that night.

Early in the morning we heard the sound of motors coming nearer and we realized that the Germans were in the city. Looking carefully out of the windows we saw in the distance long lines of greenish- grey army trucks full of soldiers driving to the centre of the city. A little later we heard through loudspeakers the following orders: "all Polish soldiers in the houses must come out immediately and surrender all arms. Not obeying this order will result in execution." We were terrified; here in our apartment we had a soldier, and although he had changed his clothing we still had to do something about his rifle, helmet, ammunition and uniform. We feared that they would seize my brother-in-law and execute him. Terrified, we waited till night time. In the middle of the night Srultche dressed himself as a woman, crossed the street, and entered the courtyard where his parents lived. They lived on the top floor. He changed clothing and then went to hide in their attic. At the same time, my brother Shloime and I snuck down to the cellar where we had hidden the night before, dug a hole in the earth floor, and buried my brother-in-law's rifle, ammunition and ammunition belt, helmet, and boots. This was a very risky undertaking because the janitor in this building was a "volksdeutsch," a German-descended Pole who would probably denounce us if he knew. After three hours of anxious fearful digging, careful not to make a noise which might draw the janitor from his first-floor apartment, we finished the task and went up to my sister's apartment.

The next day we heard from neighbours the sad news that the Germans rounded up the Rabbi and the Jewish leaders of the city, cut off their beards, and forced them to clean the public washrooms as well as to do other menial tasks. All the while they ridiculed them and took pictures for their own amusement. Later we also heard that they had seized some Jews randomly and shot them as a spectacle. The Germans were everywhere in the city and Jews were afraid to go out of their houses. Somehow we found out that a young man from Rozhan, who I knew well, was in Pultusk staying with his family. By a strange coincidence his name was Shloime Pultusker. We wanted to know what had happened in Rozhan and decided to try and go to visit him.

My brother Shloime and I walked out of my sister's apartment for the first time since the Germans had arrived. We needed to get through a number of streets before arriving at the central market place across from which this young man lived. We walked single file and as close as possible to the walls of buildings so as not to attract attention. There were no civilians to be seen, but at the market square we saw German soldiers as well as various military vehicles. Finally we arrived at our friend's house. He had a radio and was able to tell us the latest news. Poland had been overrun and was in her last throes of resistance; Warsaw was surrounded and about to capitulate. Our hometown of Rozhan, he told us, was almost 80% destroyed.

We spent only about thirty minutes with him. It was noon, and saying goodbye, we left. Again we tried to walk cautiously, single file, along buildings. Just as we had reached the other side of the market square, we were suddenly accosted by a small group of

German soldiers. "Shtehen bleiben! (stop!)" ordered the leader of the group. Suddenly we became aware that a short distance from us were some six Jewish men surrounded by a larger group of soldiers. The leader of our group ordered us to join the other Jews. When we joined the other Jews I whispered to one of them asking why they were surrounded by the German soldiers. He shrugged his shoulders and whispered back "I don't know." One of the soldiers noticed our whispered exchange and gruffly shouted, "nicht redden!" (don't speak!).

We were now eight Jewish men, the oldest possibly about 45 years old. They paired us up and had six soldiers guard us. One of the six soldiers walked to a nearby military truck, opened the back gate and removed some shovels which he gave each of us. He also removed a large, filled sack which one of us had to carry along with the shovel. We were then ordered not to speak and to march forward in the street, with three armed soldiers on each side of the column. As we marched in the street, close to the sidewalk, none of us knew where we were headed and why we were carrying shovels. Passing us slowly on the side was a column of black convertible cars with officers; when they noticed us, some of the officers laughed derisively, made gestures like cutting our throats, and shouted "tot shlagen!" (kill them!).

The sight of the officers and their gestures terrified us; we were convinced that we were carrying the shovels to dig our own graves. My mind raced ahead, there was a lump in my throat and I felt as if my heart was in a vise. And at the same time I kept asking myself silently, why only the Jews?

We marched for more than half an hour and were on the outskirts of the city. On both sides of the road there were rising green fields. The Germans talked amongst themselves but it was hard to understand what they were saying. Suddenly we were commanded to stop. They ordered us to get on the elevated green field on one side and we saw them removing their rifles from their shoulders. My mind raced ahead in fear and I thought to myself, "this is it, this is it; probably they will order us to dig our own graves. Will they cover us with the earth we dig up?" I asked myself absurdly.

As we waited, one of the soldiers addressed us, but not in as shrill a voice as earlier. "Do you know why we brought you here," he asked. "You see this field? It is a field of potatoes. Each of you has a shovel and there are potato bags in the bag that one of you is carrying. Get out there and start digging out the potatoes and fill up all the bags." We were stunned. There was an amused smirk on the soldier's face; the soldiers had deliberately made us think we were going to die. After all, they could have told us right at the start what they were going to have us do. "Now, get going!" he screamed.

We spread out and started digging. What had fooled us was the shovels. Ordinarily one didn't use shovels to dig up potatoes but rather a farm implement that looked like a ladle but with open spaces in it. I had often gone to farmers and was allowed to dig for potatoes to take home, so I too had been fooled. We hardly had time to feel any relief from the expectation of what was facing us because the soldiers, who had taken off their jackets and their ammunition belts and were sitting relaxed on a rise watching us, kept yelling "shneler,shneler" (faster, faster). After about two hours we had almost filled our bags when the same soldier who had given us the initial instruction began to scream loudly "aufheren, aufheren" (stop, stop).

We were happy to stop. It was a very hot, sunny day and we had taken off our upper garments. Soaked in sweat from our hard work we were told to do the following: we had to place each of the almost filled bags in a straight line thirty meters from each other. Now he told us that we were to dig up one potato at a time and run to our particular bag to deposit it. We didn't ask questions; we were still too afraid. To accompany this new ritual the soldiers amused themselves with an improvised ditty: "tzu eine, tzu eine, du Yiddisher shweine" (one at a time, one at a time, you Jewish swine). But some of us had not understood the last instructions which seemed senseless and we ran with a few potatoes to deposit in the bags thinking this would please the Germans. Instead, a number of the soldiers grabbed their belts and used them to beat mercilessly the offending Jews and, eventually, all of us as we tried to fulfil their orders. We couldn't understand their purpose; first they had made us work as quickly as possible and now they were absurdly making us slow down the collection of the potatoes. Like so much else that was to happen to us in the months and years ahead under the Germans, it didn't make sense. It was so offensive to see how middle aged Jews were running one after the other with single potatoes while the Germans were beating them with straps on their bare backs. The humiliation was almost more difficult to bear than the actual lashes of the belts. Who among us could imagine that the "civilized" Germans could take such pleasure in their own bullying and bestiality. We soon noticed that the sun was beginning to come down in the west and the afternoon was coming to a close. The bags were full and the soldiers were anxiously looking at their watches. They drew together and seemed to conduct a discussion about something. Later we understood what they were trying to do. They were stalling so as not to return to their company and be given a more onerous task; that's why they realized that they had to slow us down after we had almost filled the bags. Finally they ordered us to bring the filled sacks to the edge of the road. The sacks were now extremely heavy and we tried to help each other. "Nein, nein," screamed the Germans.

Everyone had to take his own sack, alone. Our shoulders and backs were still smarting from the strapping we had endured. With our last strength, each of us tried to lift our sack to bring to the road. One of us fell with his sack near the road and one of the soldiers began to kick him mercilessly with his heavy boot, screaming all the while "you dirty Jew, you don't want to work!" Fortunately, just at this moment the military truck that was to pick up the potatoes had arrived. The driver and non-commissioned officer had descended. The non-commissioned officer, probably a sergeant, in a firm, authoritative voice ordered the soldier to stop immediately and berated him for the action as was evident from the facial expression of the offending soldier. This was one of the last decent actions by a German that I was to witness during the War. Thus ended for these soldiers a "rehearsal" in how to be good Nazis.

When we had loaded the potatoes on the truck and the truck

with the sergeant and the driver had left, the soldiers who had brought us to the potato field suddenly turned to us and yelled in German "get lost." They chased us away instead of taking us back. Although puzzled, we were not slow to obey this order. We scattered in all directions. My brother Shloime and I eventually made it home just a few minutes before the military curfew began. When we entered our apartment and saw how our parents looked, we surmised how worried they had been this whole day. We were too exhausted to describe our experiences during the traumatic seven hours we had been away. My mother, seeing how we were, immediately understood that something terrible had happened to us. For the next half hour we all sat in silence around the dining room table, a silence that screamed louder than words. It was hard to accept such a humiliation, but we didn't imagine that the Germans would demean themselves so much and return to such pre-historic barbarism. I silently decided that we must leave, that we had to escape.

A few days later my father decided that he wanted to return to Rozhan to see what had happened to our home. My sister Luba declared that she would accompany father. She dressed herself as a poor older peasant woman, while my father covered his beard with a large kerchief and deliberately dressed like a poor villager. Then they left together, early in the morning. By late evening, before the curfew, they arrived in Rozhan. They were back the following evening before our own curfew and told us the following. No one bothered them on the way because they looked like impoverished beggars. When they arrived at our home they saw that it had burned down and only sections of the walls were standing. The only thing that had survived was the baking oven, but it was empty of the "chulents" we had left when fleeing. Our Polish neighbours had had a feast. My father and sister checked the cellar, and sure enough, the hole my brother and I had dug to hide our valuables was exposed and everything had been stolen. There were no Jews left in the town. My father and sister found a secluded place to bed down in the field where I and my friends used to play and, at dawn, they began the journey back. By the time they returned, they looked, indeed, as if they had aged; they didn't have to pretend.

Although we lived in great fear of going out into the streets, we decided that my older brother Shloime and I should go to Makow-Mazowietzki, twenty-one kilometres away, where our grandmother and my father's youngest sister, my aunt Esther Chane, lived with her husband and five children. We left at dawn and arrived well before noon. We stayed only an hour and responded

to our grandmother's and our aunt's admonition to return immediately to be with our parents. They were in the same plight
as we and didn't know what to do next. We said goodbye to our
grandmother and the other uncles and cousins and left. It was the
last time that we saw them; they all perished at the hands of the
Nazis.

After the war I met survivors from Makow-Mazowiecki and
they told me that very, very few Jews survived. Makow-Mazowiecki was not burned down during the initial days of the war, and
so no one fled. The Germans herded almost everyone into the
ghetto they established seven or eight months later and, then, in
1942 they were all shipped to the gas ovens of Treblinka, only 50
kilometres away. The same survivors also told me of my cousin Shloime Minoga, about a year younger than I, who was very strong
and managed to tear open the floor boards and slide out of the
wagon that was taking him to the death camp. Unfortunately there
were Polish peasants working beside the tracks during his escape.
They chased and caught him; he was turned over to the German
soldiers who automatically shot him.

My brother and I returned safely to my sister and parents
in Pultusk before the curfew. Another week or two passed and
Rosh Hashana was approaching. We hardly left the apartment.

Rumours circulated among our neighbours that the Russian army would occupy half of Poland and that we would be expelled to the other side of the River Narev which was to serve as the border between the Germans and the Russians. We encouraged ourselves with this possibility. The ten days of repentance before Yom Kippur were nearly over and my father reported that one of the neighbours who lived in the courtyard of our building would host the "minyan"(ten men required for prayer as a congregation) for Yom Kippur.

The eve of Yom Kippur arrived and we went down to the apartment of this neighbour. His windows were covered with sheets so that no one would be aware that twelve men had gathered in his apartment. We had not had the food for the traditional meal preceding Yom Kippur that helps one to endure the fast during the following day. Everyone's face appeared grey like ash and the men seemed to wrap themselves more tightly in their prayer shawls as if to shield themselves against the evil destiny that was threatening. Two small candles were flickering meekly because of the lack of oxygen in the small room. We had just completed listening to Kol Nidre when we became aware of a commotion outside. There was something approaching our building. Suddenly the door was ripped open and four or five German soldiers moved past the open door shouting "Juden Raus! Los,los, es ist nicht kein gebet haus da," (Jews out! Out, out! This is not a prayer house). They proceeded to shove us to the door with their rifles while pulling off our tallisim. My father's tallis was ripped and he was bleeding from a rifle blow to one side of his face. The other side of his face was ashen white. Everyone ran to their apartment. How did the Germans know we were praying? I guessed that the wife of the building's janitor, who was a "volksdeutsche" (a German-descended Polish citizen) had noticed a suspicious number of Jews entering the same apartment and, wanting to ingratiate herself with the occupiers, had reported us to the soldiers. Since then, whenever I celebrate Yom Kippur, I see before my eyes again that first Yom Kippur under the German occupation. It will never leave my memory.

CHAPTER 7

Eviction from Pultusk

A few days later, around seven or eight o'clock in the morning, we heard a loud commotion, screaming, and banging of doors in the corridor and even before we were able to open our door to see what was going on, the door was suddenly pushed open and a group of SS officers forced their way in. We were all frozen with fear; the only words the SS men spoke were their screams of "raus, raus." We were hardly dressed and we didn't know what to grab, clothing or food, while the Germans threatened us with their drawn revolvers and screamed constantly "shneler, shneler (faster, faster), raus, raus!" Within seconds we were in the corridor; my older, pregnant sister, Ruchl Gitl, came out last, dressed only in a night gown, house coat and slippers. They were pushing us roughly to descend the stairwell just as the others living on the other side of the stairs were also driven towards them. We couldn't think straight and were like driven animals. In the courtyard there were already other Jews driven down from their apartments in the same state as we, surrounded by the German soldiers who had forced them down. After some ten or fifteen minutes we were ordered into the street, where other Jews surrounded by Germans were already waiting. Soon the few hundred Jews who lived on the street had been gathered and were ordered to march forward in the middle of the street, guarded on the sidewalks by Germans with rifles. After about twenty minutes of marching, it became obvious that they were taking us to the city park on the edge of town. We were constantly being joined by Jews from other streets some of whom, forewarned by a few minutes, had managed to take with them small bundles of clothing and provisions. At the park we found ourselves together with a few thousand Jews, a large portion of the eight thousand Jews who lived in Pultusk. No one could answer the question of what the Germans were planning; we speculated wildly. What we did see were soldiers with machine guns surrounding us. We waited like this for hours, not being able to drink or to relieve ourselves. The day was hot. Rumours were spreading rapidly. Again we heard that Poland would be divided between Russia and Germany along the River Narev, and so the Germans were going to drive us to the other side. Each of us hoped that this rumour would prove to be true.

Finally, we noticed that the people on one side were beginning to move slowly and soon we joined the movement. By four o'clock we began to approach the other side of the park where we were funnelled through a narrow gate in the fence that surrounded this part of the park. In front of this narrow gate the Germans had set up a number of long tables behind which sat officers while soldiers with drawn weapons stood near the tables besides which, and in front, were large rain barrels and crude wooden boxes. To reach the gate we had to pass the tables where the officers demanded all our possessions and documents. We had to empty our pockets of everything and also take off rings, watches, and any jewellery we were wearing. At the end of this process, soldiers felt our clothing to make sure that we had deposited everything. My poor brother Shloime had left a tailoring thimble in his pocket. A soldier felt his pocket and noticed that he had left something and began to beat him around his face. When my brother removed the thimble and put it on the table he was beaten even more, perhaps out of disappointment that it was nothing valuable. Fortunately, he was allowed to continue with us and we were rushed through the narrow gate out of the park as soldiers screamed at us to hurry.

The scene was indescribable as thousands of people tried to escape. Soldiers were shooting into the air as we were herded toward the bridge over the Narev River: mothers with small children in their arms, older men and women trying to keep up, boys and girls old enough to be on their own, everyone was in a panic with only one thought - self-preservation. At the bridge there were more German soldiers, some lashing the panicked people with whips to force them across quicker. At the other end of the bridge was a German soldier whipping whoever passed close enough. As I approached him, slowed down by trying to help my pregnant sister, I witnessed something I was not to experience again: a German officer had just arrived and brusquely ordered the soldier to stop whipping the panicked crowd rushing past him. But it wasn't just the gesture of the officer that stayed in my memory; it was what he said to the soldier: "Halt! Halt! Ale sind doch menshen's kinder! (stop!stop! We're all children of humans)."

Half a kilometre or so from the bridge we had just crossed there was a pine forest as far as one could see. The Russians had apparently not yet arrived to occupy the eastern shore of the river. Everyone headed towards the forest to get as far away from the Germans as possible, fearful that they might change their minds. It's interesting to note human nature. As we rushed towards the forest, people split into smaller groups of families and friends. Instinct told us that we were more likely to be inconspicuous in a smaller group than in one large mass. It would also be easier to forage for food to feed a smaller group. As soon as we reached a small clearing, we sat down on the mossy portion to stop, catch our breath and consider what to do next. How close and sheltered we felt sitting in the forest on the silent earth! The herding towards the bridge was so sudden and brutal that we had had no chance to think. We were thirsty, hungry and exhausted from the events of the day with its succession of terrors. Fear had blunted our thirst and hunger, but now that the immediate terror had passed, we realized we had not eaten or drunk since the day before. We had lost everything and didn't know what the next day would bring.

Although our family sat close together, I now noticed that our small group consisted of about thirty persons, my own family of seven and some people, strangers, who had waited with us in the park and to whom we had spoken while waiting. Most were older than we. My father was still stunned from the day's terror. My mother turned to me as she had already done frequently before the war. I turned to my brother and we decided to move further into the forest while there was still light. It was already almost six and the forest would soon be dark; then we would bed down for the night. As we started walking the other people in the group followed us.

After about a half hour we found a cluster of pine trees that seemed to offer more shelter and we decided to stay there overnight. The others also found shelter nearby. I suppose they felt safer near us. When we had settled down, my pregnant sister Rochl Gitel suddenly told us something unexpected. When the Germans woke us and hurried us out of the apartment she had been the last one, not even having enough time to dress, but still dressed in her night gown, slippers and a light housecoat. As she hurried out she noticed a watch on the dining table and put it quickly in the little pocket of her housecoat. When the Germans searched everyone at the gate, they ignored her because she wasn't dressed. Imagine, till a minute earlier we owned nothing! Now suddenly we were in possession of a valuable asset. How tragically happy we were at that moment!

At the same time, we were disturbed when we remembered that my brother-in-law Srulce, Rochl Gitel's husband, was left behind hidden in the attic of the apartment building of his parents. We were afraid at what could have happened to him.

It became quite dark as night fell rapidly. In the distance we could hear occasional rifle shots. From a closer distance we heard Yiddish voices. We decided to go a little deeper into the forest hoping to be less visible and fearful that even our whispers could betray us. In a cluster of pine trees forming a sort of little circle we bedded down on the soft, moss covered earth. We decided that at dawn we would try to go further away from the bridge and the Germans. Lying on the ground and trying to grasp what had happened to us in the previous ten hours I couldn't help realizing that in less than a month I would be twenty years old. Looking around me in the darkness I could make out some of the forms of the people who had become part of our group. I realized that they were all women and children and older men. I also realized that I was the one who would have to lead the way in the morning, because I was somewhat familiar with the area from the time when I had worked for the tailor Golomb in Pultusk a year earlier.

At the first inkling of dawn I woke up and noticed the first morning light. It came from the east and I decided that was the direction we would take. No one, except the children, had to be awakened. Everyone was soon up, eager to get as far away from this place as possible. We were all still weary, but we were "lucky," having no baggage to worry about. I led my family and the others followed us at a short distance. After an hour of wandering, with the sun rising, its rays beginning to penetrate the trees, we approached the other side of the forest. From a distance we began to hear the sound of motors. We soon recognized that a few hundred meters from the edge of the forest, towards the north, there was a road. Afraid of what we would encounter, and possibly being seen in the open, we walked south at the edge of the forest and away from the road in the north.

We soon noticed blueberry bushes with matured berries along our way. We hadn't eaten or drunk anything for twenty four hours and so we began to eat the berries. A little further on, we noticed on our left vegetable fields full of matured vegetables: beautiful cucumbers, bright red radishes, white turnips, and all kinds of onions. Spreading out, we bent as low as possible and began picking the vegetables, hoping not to be spotted by anybody. After a few minutes we retreated with our treasures back into the forest. Each group sat separately and silently, and ate the things we had picked.

We realized that we must be close to a village, because vegetables are always planted not too far from farmsteads. We decided to separate into small family groups because we would be less conspicuous and it would be easier to beg for food. With the road far behind us in the north, our family began walking southeast towards a village in the distance. As we approached we heard dogs barking, but no one seemed to be outside the wooden houses. I suppose the farmers were as confused and fearful as we. We circled the edge of the village till we reached a narrow dirt road leading in a more easterly direction. Every few hours we rested. Towards evening we reached another dense forest and decided to spend the night again deep under the pine trees. Strangely, although it was already the beginning of fall, I don't remember being cold at night, perhaps because it was an unusually warm late September. Next day at dawn we were up, ate the few vegetables we had kept and continued our march eastward, away from the Germans. After a few hours of walking on the dirt road, we saw in the distance the outlines of barns and peasant huts. As we got closer and closer we noticed that there were none of the usual sounds associated with a busy village. No dogs barked, there was no mooing of cows, and not a single human voice. We approached cautiously, suspicious about the strange silence. We couldn't understand what the silence signified. My brother and I walked alone across the field towards the nearest barn, its weather-beaten wooden doors ajar. Reaching the doors, we carefully peered into the darkened barn. There was loose hay and straw, and some broken, rusty farm implements, but otherwise it was completely empty. We began to suspect that there was nobody living in the place. We walked over to the first farm hut and looked into the only small window on our side. Again it was completely empty, only a broken chair lying in the middle.

We moved to the next hut and again it was completely empty. The next barn was, like the first one, empty. We gestured to our parents and sisters, who had been waiting at the edge of the fields until we could tell them it was safe to proceed, to join us. We carefully pried open the door to another small farmhouse. Again, all that was visible were empty walls, some bottles, and strands of quarter inch string. The bottles were especially welcome because we now had something to carry drinking water and the strings were helpful because we could tie the bottles and wear them around our necks. My sister and parents went back to the fields to gather some more vegetables, radishes, cucumbers, and tomatoes, while my brother and I checked the other houses in the hope of finding something useful.

Suddenly we heard a door closing in an adjoining house. It was so deafeningly quiet that this mild sound reached us instantly. We looked out through the window towards the sound and sure enough a man was visible just coming out from a house next door. We recognized him immediately as a Polish peasant; we came outside and greeted him in Polish. He was very surprised to see us but was reassured by our Polish. He asked who we were. We both felt we could trust him and so we told our story. We thought to ourselves, what could we lose by telling the truth? He listened carefully; then we asked why all the farmhouses were empty. He told us that this village belonged to a community of "volksdu-etshe" farmers, that is, German descended Polish citizens. Since this part of the country was to be ceded to the Russians, the Germans had just yesterday evacuated the whole community. Hearing this we realized it made sense and he was telling us the truth. As we were telling him our story, I watched his face carefully to assess his reaction to our story. I decided that he was trustworthy and we could confide in him. We asked what he was doing here. He explained that he lived in a village nearby and had very little land. So for years he had been offering his services to the German farmers in return for enough produce to help feed his own impoverished family. Knowing that they had been evacuated, he had come to see what he could scrounge. He spat on the ground and grumbled "Shwabe," the derogatory Polish term for Germans. He was disappointed at the meagre pickings.

We could see that he was a poor peasant working hard to feed his family. Carefully I asked, would he be interested in earning some good money; he answered that he would do almost anything to help his family. He was a swarthy, healthy-looking man in his middle thirties. I felt that this was the right moment to tell him of our plan. We explained to him that when we were driven out of our apartment in Pultusk, our brother-in-law had remained hidden in the attic of another apartment and we were certain that he was still there (after all, we had only been away a day and a night and this morning). We told him my brother-in-law's address, where he was hiding, and how best to get there without drawing attention to himself. When he would enter the apartment, we told him to call out "Srulce" quite loudly and to say that his brother-in laws Moishe and Shloime, and his wife Ruchl-Gitel, had sent him to bring him to us. We told him that when Srulce would hear these names he would know that we had sent him and he would come with him.Of course, Srulce wouldn't leave his treasure but take it with him; thus we could pay him what would be an enormous fortune for him. If he doubted whether we would pay when he returned, he knew that he could report us to the Germans and so it wouldn't be in our interest not to pay him. We would do any-thing to stay out of the clutches of the Germans. We could see from his facial expression that the offer was attractive to him and he agreed to try. He understood that we had nothing to give him; the Germans had robbed us of everything. Pultusk was about 30 kilometres away, a distance he and our brother-in-law could cover in a full day. We told the peasant that we would wait for the next two days and one night for his return. For us the risk was that we would have to stay in one place and lose two full days of walk-

ing away from the Germans towards the Russians. But the hope

of reuniting with our brother-in-law gave us the courage to wait.

We parted with the Pole and stayed in the village. Now we had to

hope for a miracle.

For days we had not had a piece of bread in our mouths.

My brother and I decided to try and again search through the farm

houses and barns in the village to see if we could find something

to eat in addition to the vegetables we had picked. In a corner of

a barn we noticed that there were some grains of wheat spread

out on the floor. Nearby we noticed there was an ancient stone

wheat grinder, one of those that required a horse to go in circles

to move the stones against each other to grind the wheat. With

all our strength we were able to move the bar the horse would be

attached to so that we soon had a little more than a large bowl of

milled wheat. We were too exhausted to use up all the grain we

had gathered from the floor around the primitive mill. Also, the

mill made a lot of noise when we turned it so that we were afraid

our effort would attract unwelcome attention, especially because

an eerie silence reigned over the entire village. We brought the tin

bowl with the milled wheat to my mother and she baked a small

loaf of bread. Unfortunately, the sand in the milled wheat and the fact we had no salt or yeast made the bread inedible. It felt like clay in our mouths. The next day, in the late afternoon, the peasant we had sent to find my brother-in-law returned alone. He told us that on the way he was lucky to meet some peasants in their wagons going towards Pultusk and they took him along; thus he arrived in good time without having to walk too much. He found the building and Srulce's apartment and even his hiding place as we had described it. The building was completely empty and he decided to leave the city at once for there were no civilians on the streets and he was afraid the Germans would catch him. He was the only person crossing the bridge across the Narev going towards the city. The city was deserted except for one man, carrying a large parcel on his back made up of bed sheets, passing him on the bridge but walking in the opposite direction. He told us that the peasants who gave him a lift told him that rumour had it that the frontier between the Germans and the Russians was not going to be the Narev River, but the larger Bug River further east.

Hearing this, we calculated that if the "volksdeutshe," the ethnic Germans, from the village learned this they would soon be back to reclaim their village. We decided, in spite of the approaching darkness, to leave at once towards the east, to reach what would be Russian held territory. We passed some small villages and we were so hungry that we risked asking some peasants who saw us to give us some bread. And some did. From these peasants we found out that the rumours were correct: that the Germans would be occupying this area. We decided to hurry to reach the Bug River before the Germans caught up with us. We moved quickly along the narrow rutted country roads that connected one small village to the next, usually two to three kilometres apart. We thought this area was a no-mans land, but later we learned that it was already occupied by the Germans. Fortunately for us, they just had not yet come into all the villages.

CHAPTER 8

The Unwelcome Guests

Darkness fell and we could not continue. We moved to the closest forest on our right, a few hundred meters away. We bedded down in the nearest small clearing between the trees, each of us overwhelmed with the desire to reach the Bug before the Germans. It was a race between them and us, though only we were aware of it. According to the peasants we had met, we were about thirty kilometres from the life-saving river. In spite of the fact that we were weary from so many days of wandering through the fields and country roads, and our shoes were tearing (my sister Ruchl Gitel's slippers had earlier fallen apart and she was walking barefoot), we decided to rise even earlier than usual and go in the direction of the dawn leading us eastward. There the sun will rise for us and bring us hope.

We walked an entire day, passing a few villages. Around five in the late afternoon, away to the side of the last village, we passed a wooden hut. We then heard voices from inside which we recognised as Yiddish. We approached and opened the door. A group of six older women and a few children, as well as two older invalid men, were sitting or lying on the floor of the hut. Against the walls there were various self-made packs consisting of bedding. We could see that these were very plain and poor people whose Yiddish was crude. We asked them where they were from and they told us that they lived in a village near by. When they learned that the Germans were driving Jews out of the towns, they decided it was best for them to leave their houses and try to get to the Russian side. It turned out that there was another room in the hut and we decided to spend the night there. Outside the hut we had noticed a large pile of straw and we brought in as much as we needed to create some makeshift bedding for ourselves. For the first time in five nights we did not have to sleep in the open or on a hard floor.

We soon heard loud quarrelling next door. We could hear a barrage of expletives and cursing. We realised these people were somewhat crude and vulgar and we would not consider going with them. Finally they quietened and we were able to fall asleep. A few hours later, I don't know why, I woke up. Lying awake I began to think to myself about what was facing us next. We needed to go another twenty to twenty-five kilometres to the Bug River which we knew was to be the border between the Russians and the Germans, and we had heard that this coming day was when the Germans would place themselves at the western side of the river. Then nobody would be able to cross without their permission. We had to get there before the Germans. But my mother and sister were exhausted. What to do? There was no choice; we had to start soon and move on as best we could.

Suddenly I heard a noise outside; the voices were Polish with a distinct peasant accent. I noticed that my mother was also awake. I crept silently to the window and although our room was almost pitch dark, outside the bright moonlight lit up three large man just in front of the door to the shack. Their faces were quite visible and their mien not reassuring; moreover, I noticed they were each carrying a large, heavy stick. They started knocking on the door with the sticks, yelling loudly at the same time: "hey, zhidy(Jews), open the door!" Again they repeated their demand. "If you don't open the door we'll send you up in smoke!" Every-one was now up and terrified. I saw that they were going over to the nearby pile of straw and laying it around the outside walls of the hut; I realized that they meant what they said. We had to make a quick decision and I said to my parents, "I'm going out to speak to them; we have nothing to lose." It was painful to hear the collective fearful sigh, the whispered admonition not to do it, and my mother's quiet "oy." I opened the door and faced them. For a few seconds there was utter silence. The three men stared at me in the dark for a moment, puzzled that I had the courage to come out without carrying anything in my hands to defend myself.

Quietly I said to them, "Panovieh (Sirs), I know that you are looking for something valuable and I wish we had something to share with you, but we have nothing." Then I told them how the Germans had suddenly driven us out of our homes, emptied our pockets, and forced us to run east. I told them we were hungry and had nothing and I invited them to come in and see. Then I added, "what can you possibly gain by burning this shack?" There was silence for a few seconds then the middle one said,"hey, bratty (brothers), let's go." And, without saying another word, miraculously, they left.

Before the dawn even arrived we were already marching east, to the unknown. We passed little villages but in spite of hunger, we didn't stop. We were focused on only one thing - to reach the border before the Germans. We were unshaven, bedraggled, our clothing was torn. We washed ourselves wherever we found some water. In short, we looked like beggars. The only thing I carried was a bottle on a string around my shoulder on one side.

Around noon we passed a larger village. We inquired of some Polish farmers the direction towards the River Bug. Seeing the shape of my mother and sister, and that it was getting difficult for them to continue, we also asked if anyone was willing to take us to the river, some ten to twelve kilometres away, in a horse-drawn cart. They were reluctant. A few meters away stood a tall farmer with a whip in his hand. Hearing our conversation he came closer and asked how we would pay him if he was to take us to the river. We answered that the only thing we possessed was a watch that had cost 23 zlotys, a significant sum then. He asked to see it and my brother took it out of his pants pocket and handed it to him. He examined it carefully while we were waiting for the good news that he would take us to the River. Suddenly, he turned around and ran towards his wagon and horse nearby. The farm wagon was flat because it was unloaded and so the Pole sat himself sideways on the nearest side and began whipping the horse which began pulling the wagon.

Startled by what was happening, I threw off my bottle and began, with all my energy, racing after the wagon which was now picking up speed. When the Pole saw me coming alongside he tried whipping me. I realized that the way to avoid the whip was to run as closely to the wagon as possible. Since the whip was long, by running close to him he wouldn't be able to reach me. I wanted to reach him and pull him down by his hanging feet. Just as I reached him he kicked me in the chest, I lost my balance, fell sideways, and the rear left wheel ran over the side of my forehead. My family was terror-stricken, witnessing what had happened as they were running behind me. But I had not lost consciousness and I noticed that the Pole, seeing all the blood on my face, become frightened and threw down the watch. I had the presence of mind to run over to where it lay and to pick it up even before my family reached me. My left forehead had a long cut which was bleeding profusely. Seeing me bleeding so badly, my parents were convinced that I had sustained a serious wound. But I was able to assure them that I was alright and remind them that in two hours we would be at the Bug and I would get care on the other side. They soon found some water to wash the wound and my face. But the watch was still in our hands.

We began to believe that we would reach the river in time. With our last strength we marched towards the river, deciding not to take another chance with the peasants. After a few hours we glimpsed the river in the distance and that gave us a last spurt of energy. Arriving at the western shore, we experienced a lucky break. Not far from where we were standing, we noticed a beached empty rowboat with the oars still in it. No one was close by. We pushed it into the water, all seven of us got in almost tipping the boat, and we carefully and slowly rowed the short hundred or so yards across to freedom from fear. Thus, we left the painfully tragic western shore of the Bug. I was not to see it again till forty-seven years later.

CHAPTER 9

On The Soviet Side

In less than half an hour we reached the eastern side of the River Bug. Russian soldiers helped us out of the little rowboat. Never, never will I forget the moment when I realized that only an hour earlier we had been hunted like animals and now we were being welcomed with friendliness in a secure place, with food and medical attention provided to us. My injured forehead, with the rag soaked in blood now slowly drying, received immediate attention from a Russian medic. Fortunately, my wound had not been deep, but I had to wear a bandage for the next two weeks. Nothing can erase the human treatment we received from the Soviet authorities at that crucial time. The area we had reached was a small town named Tchizev, close to the larger city of Zambrov. In Tchizev, there were already thousands of Jewish "bezences" (refugees) like us, uprooted from their towns and shtetls in Poland. Through loudspeakers the Russian authorities pleaded that the refugees go to the railway station to board trains to Bialystok, a much larger city, because in this little town there was no way to provide shelter.

That same evening we spoke to hundreds of our fellow refugees and each had his own horror story. To whomever we spoke, we told them that we had left my brother-in-law Srulce Ziskind behind and asked that if by any chance they were to meet up with him, to tell him that his family went to Bialystok. Almost everybody we spoke to was in a similar situation and had also lost relatives whom they hoped to find on this side of the frontier.

In the makeshift marketplace that had developed in the town, Russian soldiers went around asking people if they had watches for sale. This was our cue because our only possession of any value was the watch that I had managed to rescue. I replied to one of the soldiers that we had a watch to sell. I showed it to him and he asked me how much I wanted for it. Knowing that the official price for a Polish zloty was one Russian rubble, I told him I wanted 50 rubbles, expecting that he would refuse because I knew the watch had only cost 23 zlotys. Imagine my surprise when he took out 50 rubbles and paid me for the watch. Later I found out that the black-market prize for a zloty was four rubbles. But at least we had some money to tide us through. We received bread and a few other foodstuffs from the Red Army, which did its best under such difficult circumstances to feed everyone. Also, the Jewish community in the town had established a soup kitchen for the refugees. We ate and that night we slept on the floor of a non-descript public building.

In the early morning we went with hundreds of others to the train station and boarded a train for Bialystock. I will always remember the friendly welcome of the Red Army in Tchizev; we didn't have to pay for anything, not even the fare to Bialystok. By lunchtime we were in Bialystock. Freight trucks were waiting for us at the train station and they took us to various public buildings, movie theatres, churches, organizational locals, where they registered us and told us that we couldn't stay in Bialistok because thousands of refugees were arriving daily and there was no more space for them. We, however, decided that we would try to stay in the city in the hope of meeting up with my brother-in-law. We kept asking people arriving from Tchizev whether they had seen a man matching our description of Srulce. And then the miracle; some people did, indeed, respond that they had met such a man and that he was inquiring of everyone about meeting a family called Gruda. A few days later there was a day of tears and happiness. We had been moving from group to group inquiring and on the third day, lo and behold, there was Srulce, sitting on the ledge of a building with his tied up bundle of clothing and blankets. You can imagine the joy we all felt on finding each other.

He told us the following. When he was in hiding in the attic in Poltusk he managed to avoid the round up; in fact he was able to see part of it from his vantage point. On the third day he decided to pack up some clothing and blankets and all his valuables and try to get to the bridge we had crossed three days earlier. No one bothered him. The Germans, believing there were no more Jews left in Poltusk, assumed he was a Polish peasant. He crossed the bridge without a problem and, more or less, followed the same route to the Bug River we had taken a few days earlier. A peasant on the way had told him that Russia and Germany had divided Poland and that the Russians occupied the other side of the River Bug. This way he, too, reached Bialystock, though in a lot better shape physically and financially than we. Now we were together once more.

It was a very disturbed time; people were constantly looking for relatives. Thus, it was possible to share all kinds of news and information. Srulce, my brother-in-law, had met people who told him that in Lomza, about 50 kilometres away and also under Russian occupation, there was work available in his trade as a plasterer, and he decided to go there with our pregnant sister.

In the meantime, the authorities didn't want these thousands of refugees to crowd Bialystok and urged us to go deeper into Russia. We didn't want to go to Lomza, remembering our experience there from 1928-32. We decided therefore, to join hundreds of other refugees on their way to Pinsk, about 200 kilometres south east of Bialystok. Around the middle of October we arrived in Pinsk, a city formerly in Poland but, after the War, incorporated into Byelorussia.

When we arrived there were already significant numbers of refugees, but not as many as in Bialystok. We were billeted in public places like school halls and theatres. We bathed in public baths and there were soup kitchens where we were fed, at least minimally. While we were in these public places, we were harangued by political commissars to remember that we had been rescued from the Polish yoke by the motherland, Russia. Of course, no mention was made of the Russo-German pact in late August to divide Poland. Much of the propaganda promised that the father of the Soviet Union, Comrade Stalin, would provide for us. We were never comfortable with being dependents; we were always used to working and maintaining ourselves. We decided not to wait for Comrade Stalin to help us and after four or five days we began to look for work. My brother Shloime found work in his trade with a men's tailor and I found work as a labourer in a lumber yard. There were no power tools or vehicles in the yard and everything was done with elbow grease. We had to cut wood with handsaws and to carry the raw logs and the finished boards on our shoulders or backs. After two or three weeks I was lucky and found work at a private ladies' tailoring shop. I still remember the owner's name, Michal Kolodny. For a while, with both my brother and I working, life took on a little normalcy. However, since the Russians had occupied this part of Poland, there were soon shortages in everything. They had requisitioned many of the larger factories and other large-scale enterprises and destroyed the initiative to produce more since there was no reward for it. In spite of this I was still grateful to the Russians for having rescued us from the murdering Germans.

I don't remember how we found an apartment in a suburb of Pinsk. It was in a wooden house on an unpaved street. My father found work in his shoe-making trade; in such conditions, with few people able to afford new shoes, repairing older ones was a valuable skill. Life became somewhat "normal."

There were no fortunes to be made in my shop. My boss, Kolodny, though a sympathetic and kind man in his middle thirties, had a beautiful but terribly shrewish wife, constantly angry and abusive. He had found her in Shedlitz while serving in the Polish army. After military service he married her and brought her home to Pinsk. However, it needs a Sholem Aleichem to describe the scene that met me every morning.

Since they had two small children, my master would be occupied in the morning with cleaning, dressing and feeding the infants while we had to wait until he could turn his attention to the work. All this time his loud wife would be busy gossiping with the neighbouring women or primping to maintain her good looks. There were sometimes pitiful but comic scenes as customers waited while Kolodny would beg her to take over with the children so he could work; she just ignored him. The consequence was that I wasn't earning much money.

In those early months of the war it was still possible to smuggle across the frontier between the Germans and the Russians. Some people endangered themselves by going back to bring relatives, others to make money. Suddenly my master's wife got it into her head that she wanted to go see her parents in Shedlitz, now occupied by the Germans. We tried to dissuade her, stressing the extreme danger she would be exposing herself to if she crossed. She wouldn't listen; one day she packed and left, leaving her hapless husband to look after the children. He became virtually paralysed from the worry and almost stopped taking on new work. Many days I would come to work for only one or two hours. Finally, after seven worrisome weeks she suddenly appeared, none the worse for wear. And although she didn't stop talking about her experiences and what she had seen, we couldn't find out what she had actually done and how she had managed to survive her ordeal.

The winter of 1939-40 was not too severe so it was easier to survive even though we didn't have enough winter clothing or bedding. In Pinsk there was a Jewish women's welfare organization which helped us with some clothing. We strove to adjust to our conditions and to live as normal a life as possible under the circumstances. Finally, we received a letter from my sister that she was close to giving birth. My mother decided to go to Lomza to help her, though it was not an easy undertaking. In January my sister gave birth to a baby girl who was named Luba. A few days later I too left for Lomza in order to bring my mother back to Pinsk.

What had happened to my oldest brother Itche Nussn, six years older than I.? He had completed his service in the Polish army in 1936. He wanted to make "Alyia"(immigration) to Palestine, so immediately after being demobilized he went on Hashomer Hatzair "hachshara," a system of group living on the model of a kibutz to prepare him to live on a real kibutz in Palestine. Even before entering the army he had spent a year in "hachshara." By 1938 he was eligible to receive an immigration certificate, but not being sufficiently aggressive, he let someone else in the movement precede him. When the war broke out, he was in a "hachshara" group in Grodno and married his girlfriend, from Lomza, who was a member in the same group. My mother was a little disappointed that her oldest son had married without the family, but the war had separated us. As soon as he learned that we were in Pinsk he joined us with his now pregnant wife, Sara (born Rogoza). My brother had given years to the Zionist movement but someone higher up took his place and he was cheated out of his reward of going to Palestine and helping to create the State of Israel. In Pinsk he was soon able to get a position as a driver for the municipality, a very good job which allowed him to be reasonably comfortable. A boy, Nachman, was born to the couple in Pinsk sometime in July or August, but by May, in the Spring, the rest of our family was forced to leave Pinsk and we were not there at his birth.

My brother was a handsome man, very kind and good-hearted, liked by everyone. After we were separated for the second time I tried for many years to find out what had happened to them. Only lately, through the diligence of my son living in Israel have I learned of my brother's fate. My son, through the good offices of the Israeli Association of Pinsker survivors, found out that there was a list of the names of those Pinsker who had survived the first elimination of the Pinsker Ghetto in July, 1942. He, his wife Sara, and young son Nachman are on that list. In October of that year they were murdered along with the other survivors during the final liquidation of the Pinsker Ghetto.

CHAPTER 10

Sernik, Winter 1939-40

The Russian authorities ordered all who had come from the German side of Poland to register with the NKVD, the Russian secret police. The announcement was posted in all open spaces. When we spoke to people who had already registered, they told us that the NKVD demanded to know the following: do you want to return to your hometown on the other side, where the Germans are, or do you want to get a Russian passport and become a Russian citizen? And they demanded a decision in a few days. Understandably this caused the "Bezences" (refugees from the other side) all kinds of worries. A lot of people had left family there, others couldn't imagine that Germans would destroy the Jews because didn't Germany have a non-aggression pact with Russia? And seeing the corruption under the Soviet regime, a lot of people didn't know what to do, whether to accept a Russian passport or to return home? It was a serious question. No one could imagine then that Germany would destroy a whole people – Germany, a country of great culture, of great philosophers and literature and composers. People thought that they would adjust to the new conditions and at least be at home. Those who had already suffered under the Germans had an easier time making a decision not to return. But those who had escaped their home before the Germans arrived could not believe what they were told of German brutality, and so quite a number signed up to go back.

When the question was put to us, I remember quite well that our father wanted to return and we had trouble persuading him. He remembered World War I when they had to evacuate themselves from Rozhan deeper to the East (at the time Poland didn't exist) and when he came with his family to the region of Pinsk, he had a lot of problems with the Russians. For example, when he prayed on his wagon outside, wearing his tfilin(phylacteries), the Russians accused him of wearing some apparatus of spying and communicating with the enemy. Our discussion with father now was very heated. I told him that I would not register to go back. It took a while, but finally he gave in.

A few days later we all went to the office of the NKVD to register to become Soviet citizens and ask for Russian passports. After a few questions a police officer told us that we would get Russian passports but that we wouldn't be allowed to live in large cities, nor in any area less than fifty kilometres of the frontier with the Germans because we were not born in the liberated Polish territories. The authorities gave us a few months to find a new residential area. In the meantime they provided us with temporary documents and promised that we would receive the passports later. Speaking with various people in Pinsk about smaller towns in the vicinity, I remembered having heard even before the War about a small town called Motele, the birthplace of Chaim Weizman, eventually the first president of Israel. One acquaintance in Pinsk told us that he had a good friend in a small town called Sernik, about forty kilometres away, and he was certain we would be welcome there as there was a lack of tailors and shoemakers and the peasants in the area paid with produce from their farms so one did not have to rely on government stores with their shortages. Also, there was a Jewish community there and this appealed to us. The problem was, however, that to get to Sernik was not so simple because there was no proper road and one had to get there by boat over the River Pina. In winter, when the river froze up, you could get across on sleds. But it was already the spring of 1940, with the famous Pinsker mud, and the ice on the lake was breaking up and melting. We wanted to get to Sernik as soon as possible because there was no work in Pinsk and life was very difficult.

One early morning in May I walked over to the little port. My brother was still working, but there was no work for me with Kolodny. It was a beautiful, sunny day and I rented a rowboat to row to Sernik up the river. By evening time, rowing against the current, I arrived in Sernik. I had with me a little letter from the man who had advised us to go to his friend in Sernik, urging him to help us in whatever way he could. The main thing was that I needed to find a place to live. I asked around to find the man to whom the letter was addressed and I found him. He was a good-hearted man and invited me to sleep over at his house. He also told me about Sernik. He reiterated what his friend had told us: that here in Sernik we would find a lot of work because the peasants sought tradesmen. He also told me that he knew of a hut made up of one large room available for rent. We went over to the owner, and knowing that there was no housing in Sernik, I rented the hut. I was very pleased that I had succeeded in finding living quarters. In the corner of the large room there was a primitive brick oven like in all the peasant huts. I slept over a second night at my new friend's house, and early in the morning I went back to the boat and began rowing to return to Pinsk. Now, rowing with the current, it was a pleasure.

I came back and told my family the good news that we had

a place to live and that we could leave Pinsk. We had virtually no furniture and little clothing, so we were light passengers. However, we did posses a sowing machine, our treasure. We purchased tickets for the little steamboat, then said goodbye to my brother Itche-Nussen and his wife who decided to remain in Pinsk. Before leaving Pinsk, we heard the sad news of what had happened with those people who had registered to return to their homes where the Germans were. The NKVD gathered them up, put them in freight trains, and shipped them to Siberia and beyond. Thousands perished in the work camps from hunger, hard work, and disease. It's also true that had they returned to their homes, they would have suffered the same fate as those who ended up in the death camps. However, about 150,000 survived in Siberia and eventually left Russia after the war.

Finally we were on our way to Sernik. When we arrived, we had to hire a carpenter to build some beds and tables for us. It was hard at first, but it didn't take long for the peasants to find out that tradesmen had arrived and they brought us their hand-crafted linen and material to make clothing for them. Even our father had work because the peasants made leather from the skins of their animals and wanted it turned into boots. We were paid with produce; we soon had in our room flour, honey, all kinds of grains, eggs, and greens, even chickens. We had a lot of work and plenty to eat. All we needed to buy was salt and naphtha or kerosene for the lamps. On Sabbath we attended "shul" and slowly we made friends. There were a few "shtibls" (prayer rooms in private homes) and one shul. After a few months we received a letter from Lomza from my sister Ruchl-Gitl and Srulce. My brother-in-law's work contract had finished and they had decided to join us in Sernik. We were very happy that we would have them with us with their little daughter, Luba. We found a place for them to live. It was a long trip for them, from Lomza to Bialystok, then Brisk, then Pinsk and finally with the steamboat to Sernik. When they arrived, my brother-in-law didn't have to wait long to secure a lengthy contract to plaster soldiers' barracks in a neighbouring town.

Our life became relatively normal. This was now the summer of 1940. In spite of the fact that war was raging in Western Europe we didn't feel it. I was working so hard that I hardly had the time to read a newspaper or a book. As well, the fact is that I still had difficulty reading Russian. The town of Sernik was like a big village. There were only a few unpaved streets with one story buildings. Most of the Jews were involved in trading farm animals and horses and also fish which they bought from the White Russian peasants. However, when the Soviets captured this area they began to propose creating collective farms, Kolhozes, and this created a stir among the peasants who were obviously opposed. When they used to come to bring us work, they complained bitterly about the prospect. However, the Russian authorities still had many problems in other areas, so they had not yet forced collectivization on the peasants.

One day, a tall heavy set man, very well dressed, entered our one room home and workshop. He introduced himself as Duchin and he wanted us to do some tailoring for him. Looking around sceptically, he asked if we were capable of doing finer work with better materials. We assured him that we were good tailors from Poland but that there was no demand here for finer work. Later he and his son, once they had assured themselves of the quality of our work, gave us substantial orders. We became friendlier and they began to trust us. He told us that he was from Pinsk where he had owned the largest plywood factory in Poland. The Russians confiscated his factory and forced him to leave the city; he was lucky not to have been jailed as a capitalist. They confided to us that they were seeking a way to leave Russia altogether. They came often and we had very interesting discussions with them. The son, who was about 28, was educated and very intelligent, speaking a number of languages including German, Russian and, of course,

Polish. They were hoping to go to Vilna which at that time had been returned to Lithuania and was not yet occupied by the Russians. From there they hoped to emigrate even further. The son explained to us that in reading between the lines in the Russian papers, he could discern criticism of Germany and that the "friendship" between Germany and Russia was dissipating quickly; they would probably be at war soon. The son advised us to think about this. After this last conversation, in fact, we didn't see them again; they left.

That summer we were very busy with work and managed to save some funds. Everything seemed good, but I couldn't forget my last conversation with Mr. Duchin when he had warned me that if war would break out between Germany and Russia, we would not be able to escape from Sernik. Through the summer and the following winter this warning haunted me. The regional authority for Sernik and other small towns and villages in the vicinity was the larger town of Visotsk some 50 kilometres south east of Sernik. In July we suddenly received a notice from the regional authority in Visotsk that we have to come there to receive our Russian passports.

My sister Ruchl-Gitl and her husband were not required to go as they had received their Russian passports when in Lomza.

That summer was hot and dry, so we hired a peasant with a horse and cart and set ourselves on the dirt road to Visotsk. The road led through a number of villages. About ten kilometres before Visotsk the road had narrowed and flattened, with swampy ground on both sides. The cart moved slowly, with my mother sitting at the back of the cart and the rest of us walking alongside on each side. Suddenly, in the distance ahead of us there appeared a motorized van. The farmer started crossing himself in panic and confessed that his horse had never encountered a motorized vehicle. When I stopped looking at the approaching van, I saw the horse rearing upward with the attached cart and my mother about to be thrown violently from the back of the cart. In a split second I had the instinct to rush over and lift my mother out of the back of the cart. When the horse came down on its forelegs for a moment, the peasant quickly covered its head with a horse blanket and held his head closely to him as the van passed us on the narrow road. Thus I was able to avoid a serious mishap to my mother.

Finally, we arrived at the regional authority in Visotsk. Our passports were ready at the NKVD headquarters. When they gave us the passports they told us that we were now Russian citizens but to read the statute in the passport that specified we were not to reside in any large city nor within 50 kilometres of the German-

Russian border.

We already knew about these restrictions from our time in Pinsk when they had given us the temporary passports. The trip back went without incident. We were pleased that now we were no longer nameless, stateless refugees.

CHAPTER 11

Before The Storm

In the same year, November 1940, I received a notice from the military authorities that I have to report to the Visotsk regional military commission for mobilization into the Red Army. From Sernik and the region around there were more than 20 young men with the same year of birth as I, 1919. Understandably, my whole family was worried, but there was no alternative; I had to report. My date to report was early January, 1941. Everyone had to report with hair completely cut. Very early one morning we gathered in front of the town's civic building and got into three large, open farm sleds for the trip to Visotsk. We were only two Jewish men among the White Russian boys; the other Jewish boy was a native of Sernik. All the peasant boys wore sheepskins against the freezing cold, but I was bundled up well and we also had rough blankets provided with the sleds. As well, we sat close together for warmth. It was still dark, the sky clear and full of stars as we passed the dark outlines of forests. Two hours after leaving, we stopped in front of a small farmhouse in a little village. The old babushka welcomed us into her front room and asked: "Rebiata (children), where are you going?" When we told her that we were going to a military commission in Visotsk to be mobilized, she put her hands to her cheeks and with a worrisome look on her face intoned in a White Russian dialect, "Oy Rebiata, Bude Vina (there will be war)." After a cup of hot water (kipyiatok) we got on the sleds again and with nostalgic White Russian songs continued our journey to Visotks. After a while each of us took out some of the food his family had provided to have a bit of "breakfast."

We arrived at the military command, in Visotsk, on time and reported to the military commander. He looked over the names and commenced a roll call. Another officer, a major, took us immediately outside for exercises: stretching, knee bends, running in formation, and how to fall and then rise rapidly from a falling position. After about an hour of this, the major put us into formation and commenced a patriotic speech about how happy we should feel about being in Russia and participating in the defence of "Matushka Russia," the Russian motherland. Then he took us back into the military headquarters, to a large room which was the "health commissariat" to determine our physical condition. We had to strip completely to be examined by a number of doctors, one of whom I recognized as being from Sernik. He remarked to me his wonder that considering the swamps around Sernik, the youth were in such good physical shape, all hardy, broad shouldered peasant boys. Among the doctors were a number of women, and I found it extremely difficult to find myself completely naked in front of them. This was the first time I had ever been in such a situation. They all went about their business without emotion or a smile, tapping our chests and backs, measuring our height, asking us to breathe heavily and so forth.

After all the formalities, we were led into another room where we waited to be called by the commander to be given the appropriate papers to report for duty. When it was my turn I entered the commander's office. He looked me over and then said: "physically you are completely acceptable to the Red Army, but there is a problem; since you were born on the German-occupied side of Poland, you are technically a refugee and cannot be accepted." Then he wrote across, in large letters, on my document: "bezenec" (refugee).

By nightfall we were back in Sernik. Needless to say, none my family regretted that I had been rejected by the Red Army. Now we were looking forward to winter ending and being able to implement our plans to move to a larger centre where there would be trains and highways so that we could escape if the situation demanded. Around the middle of May my brother-in-law and I set out to Dombrowitz, a city about 50 kilometres distant which had a train station. Passing some peasants on the dirt road, we asked if they knew of a shorter way to Dombrowitz. They told us that if we were not fearful, we could shorten our route by fifteen kilometres by crossing a certain forest on the other side of which there was swamp.

They gave us directions about how to cross the swamp safely. Firstly, they warned us not to cross the swamp where the water level was very low, because there the mud is quite loose and one can sink easily; in fact, we must choose those sections of the swamp where the water looks like a lake, in some places being a meter deep, because there the pressure of the water has made the ground underneath a lot firmer. Naturally we would have to strip and carry our clothing above the water.

The day was beautiful as we set out in the direction the peasants had suggested. To ensure that their advice and direction had been true, we asked other peasants along the way and received identical instructions, warning us to be careful.

After some hours going through the forest, we did, indeed, reach a swamp. We took a short rest and then evaluated our situation. We tried the swamp by gingerly putting a foot into the low water. Sure enough, within a few centimetres it became difficult to pull our feet out. We therefore walked along the edge of the swamp until we reached a section where the swamp did, indeed, look like a lake. Again we tried the swamp; although the water seemed muddy, it was possible with a little effort to pull a foot out to make the next step. We undressed, made bundles we could carry on our heads, and slowly began moving forward in the swamp. The abnormal walk took about an hour, but it was worth it, because afterwards we learned that we had saved ourselves almost twenty kilometres. When we told other peasants about our route they marvelled at our daring. A few hours later we found ourselves at the train station in Dombrowitz where we bought tickets to Sarny. I don't recall were we spent the night, perhaps in the station – a common sight all over Russia then – but the following morning we took the train to Sarny. There we encountered Jews; there was an established community. We enquired about finding housing and were directed into town where there were single family huts, and we managed to rent two. After sleeping the night, we retraced our route home and arrived the next evening.

We completed the work which we had accepted and began to make preparations to leave Sernik. By the end of May, having hired a farm wagon with two horses, our whole family including my sister and brother-in-law and their little daughter, set off on the road to Dombrowitz, passing through many villages and we sometimes changed to other country roads to circle the swamps we had crossed by ourselves. Because we had left very early in the morning, we were able to arrive by the evening. We went directly to the train station and boarded the first train we could get to Sarny. After arriving, it took us a week to settle in the two huts we had rented. It didn't take long to get work, in striking contrast to the hardship in Pinsk.

The conversations with the people we came into contact with were tense and not very clear. One group maintained that there would soon be war with Germany; others, following the official line, contended that the two countries had very good relations, and besides, why would Germany want to start a second front with Russia when she was fighting in the west with England and France. However, everywhere there was fear and confusion.

Three weeks passed from the time of our arrival in Sarny and it was June the 21; Germany suddenly invaded Russia. The radio blared assurances that the Red Army would smash the fascist enemy. At the same time we could see the officials loading trucks and leaving for the East; this created a panic in the population and the result was soon utter chaos.

CHAPTER 12

War

June 21, 1941, was a beautiful sunny day, a day that reminded me of September 1, 1939. The loudspeakers blared that the fascist hordes had invaded the fatherland. The same confusion reigned among the population, but with one significant difference. In 1939, when the Germans invaded Poland, the Polish population didn't try to leave; this time, even many non-Jews began the trek east to escape the invaders. At this point I want to explain that previously when I tried to describe our parting from our parents in Sarny, whenever I started to write I would become virtually powerless, because this is one of my most tragic memories about what happened to my family. I just couldn't find the strength and would postpone it for another time. But now I have no choice since I'm writing my autobiography; I have to find the emotional strength to deal with our departure from our parents, painful though it is to recall. The day the Germans invaded, June 21, will never leave my memory; it was the day my brother Shloime, my brother-in-law

Srulce, and I left my parents in Sarnay. How did it happen? It is now 64 years since it happened and it still haunts me. I remember that we proposed to our parents that we all leave the house where we had moved in only three weeks earlier. We felt that the Germans would soon arrive, so we suggested that we go as soon as possible to the train station and go east into Russia itself. Our father was adamantly opposed, saying "I have run enough. I have no more strength to run. Whatever will happen to all the Jews will also happen to us." It was tragic; we couldn't convince him. He said, "you are young, but we? We have no strength to start again to wander." My father was then only 53, and my mother added, "if father doesn't go neither will I." Then my sisters added that if our parents weren't going, they would also not go, especially with a small child yet. When I think often of this moment, I can't forgive myself: why didn't I try harder to convince them; why wasn't I more stubborn and forceful? I feel even now that had I insisted more assertively, I could have changed their minds. As I write this now, it seems to me still that I must tell them once more that they 'must' come with us…but no one is there; only my imagination is haunting me. When I consider how much pain and suffering they went through – if only from missing us – my heart tightens like a vise. I feel guilt as the author of their suffering and carry a wound in my heart. We said goodbye...I have to stop because my tears choke my heart. Till the end of my life this will haunt me. We parted in front of the house and hurried to the railway station which was nearby. Luckily, or perhaps unluckily, a freight train was standing in the station already full of people sitting on the open wagons. Before we knew it we were sitting among them. A moment later the whistle blew and the train began moving.

The people already sitting on the flatcar were mostly young families and Russian speaking. The day was very beautiful, but our feelings were very sombre. The train rolled on and there was no stopping for a long time. People near us on the flatcar who were familiar with the area told us that the next large station would be at the earlier border between Poland and Russia at a city called Shepatofka. After three or four hours at a steady pace, the train suddenly began to slow down. From both sides of the tracks we could see forests in the distance. The train stopped. Suddenly we saw and heard a number of aeroplanes that circled low over our train. In a few seconds we heard explosions nearby; everyone jumped off the train and ran towards the forests. Looking back we saw more explosions and fire clouds reaching into the sky. We dropped to the ground and heard volleys of machine bullets whistling over our heads. We lay still quite a while until the shooting stopped. We see the train still intact and then heard the shrill whistle of the locomotive. Everyone began to run back to the train and we followed them. Back on the flatcar we heard that the Germans dropped parachutists nearby. That's why we were also attacked, to create havoc behind the Russian lines. The train picked up speed and travelled faster than before. There is no question of stopping at Shepatofka now. It began to get darker and we continued on for a couple of hours. The train began to slow down. In the darkness we could see the outlines of houses but no lights; it is war, and lights were forbidden. We were approaching the capital of the Ukraine, Kiev.

CHAPTER 13

Kiev

It was completely dark when the train finally stopped in Kiev. We went into the large hall in the railway station together with hundreds of other refugees. We were used to it already. With everyone else we lay down on the cement floor and got some sleep. Early in the morning we noticed people were going purposefully in one direction. We asked them where they were headed and were told "to the Tolchok." This was the local flea-market; the nearby stores were closed, having no goods to sell and the only place where it might be possible to buy something was at this flea- market. Arriving at the market, we saw what people were selling: a string, a chair, every little thing was for sale. This was understandably the free market: old clothes, used shoes, used pots and dishes, and also some new things which people had purchased in the government stores and were now selling for four or five time what they had paid for them. You could recognize that the Soviet regime had sucked out the marrow from the citizens of this huge country.

Nevertheless, the Russians hated invaders, and I could feel that the majority of citizens were united against the German enemy.

We managed to buy something to eat and we decided that we had to leave Kiev as quickly as possible. We could hear the sound of German planes high above the skies of Kiev. We got back to the train station and found out from people that there was a train leaving for Dniepropetrovsk, a big city quite a way east from Kiev. As we listened to the public loudspeakers broadcasting the news from the battlefields, one could tell that the Russian army was suffering defeat in spite of the repetitive claims that it was undefeatable. We sensed that they were retreating on all fronts. On the train station we saw arriving trains full refugees from the west, all looking to escape even further east. Speaking to people waiting like us we heard only one thing: that the enemy was advancing with tremendous speed. The Russian army in the meantime was burning and destroying everything in its path as it retreats so it doesn't fall into the enemies hands.

We were able to get on the train going to Dniepropetro-vsk. Understandably, no one was buying tickets and the train was packed with people. There were whole families with small children and also elderly people on the train. We travelled packed like sardines a whole night and everyone was deep into his own thoughts. Every so often I felt a pang in my heart, wondering what our parents and sisters were doing, but the train was going further and further from them. In the early dawn when the train stopped at a station for a few minutes, people ran out of the wagons to get boiled water, "kipyatok," which was available for free in nearly all stations. This became the warm meal available to us. But it was still better than being at the mercy of the Germans. After half a day we arrived in the suburb of a great industrial city. One could see many factory chimneys; it was, after all, the crown jewel of Russia's heavy industry. When one spoke with people about Dniepropetro-vsk, one could feel their great pride, especially the construction of the huge electric dam that gave the Soviet Union an enormous leg up in their efforts at industrialization. When the train stopped at the train station we three descended carrying our little bundles. We didn't know what to do next. We left the station and looked around in the streets. We noted that the people walking past us looked well fed and better dressed than we had seen in the last few weeks. As we stood wondering where to go next, we noted that a middle aged man was walking towards us. For a moment he stopped and observed us, and then asked us in Russian where we were from. We answered him in Russian; from our reply he recognized that we were not Russians and he likely realized that we were Jews. He asked us, in a very nice Yiddish, "are you Jews?" Understandably we were very happy to hear the question, and we told him in Yiddish where we came from. He told us that he had lost his wife not long ago and he lived alone in a large house; then he invited us to stay with him as long as we wanted. As we listened to him, we could hardly believe what we were hearing. Seeing us astounded, he said "let's go." We followed him to an attractive, wide street and a large, clean house. He opened the door into a spacious hall out of which radiated large, well-furnished rooms. We could hardly believe what we were seeing. After we stepped in, he told us: "lay down your bundles, and before anything you will have warm showers. Then you'll eat and we will talk." It seemed to us like a dream. After emerging from showering and dressing ourselves in the few clean garments we still had, he invited us into his dining room, a room with a large, heavy table. He put down plates of boiled eggs, milk, jam and fresh bread. Then he poured each of us and himself a glass of tea from a samovar standing on a credenza on one wall. As we ate he asked us about our families and trades, and what had happened to us in the last few weeks. We told him in detail what had transpired with us since the Germans had invaded our town and how they behaved towards the Jews in the occupied towns. He listened very carefully, his face showing that he could hardly believe our descriptions and our story of escape; we had to repeat our descriptions more than once till he would accept them. Finally, after a pause he told us that he would have no difficulty finding work for us because he knew many people who wouldn't refuse him. When he told us what his occupation was, we could understand why. He was a supplier of meat to the Red Army in the Dniepropetrovsk area. He decides how much cattle each "Kholhoz" (collective farm) must supply. Thus he lacked nothing and this was obvious from the condition of his house and the table he set before us.

After our story, he told us that if he had to abandon his house to flee, he would first destroy it with a grenade. He was obviously a generous man with a good heart, and without children and his wife recently deceased, he wanted in some way to help the needy, especially Jews. He was a well-built, strong man, a bit on the heavy side, but energetic and enterprising, but with a very pleasant, reassuring face.

That night we went early to bed; our benefactor had shown us each to a separate bed. What luxury! We were exhausted from so many days and nights on the trains, without even having undressed. Probably we fell asleep instantly.

Suddenly, we woke to thunderous explosions shaking the

house. It was in the middle of the night. At first we were disoriented, each asking "what happened!" We ran out into the hallway
where we saw our host who was even more disoriented than we.
We could hear the distant humming of the waves of messershmit
bombers attacking Dniepropotrovsk for the first time. Almost instantly we three made the decision forced on us by the bombers;
we would go east in the morning. We told our host, "if the German
bombers could reach even Dniepropetrovsk, then we can't stay
here." Our host was besides himself; how was it possible that the
Red Army had allowed the German planes to reach even this far. It
was a huge puzzle for him and also a terrible disappointment. He
was a fine, simple man and I regret to this day that I have forgotten
his name. Next morning we regretfully prepared to leave such a
special person, but we felt that the enemy would flood a lot of territory and we had to escape as quickly and as far as possible.

Our host felt beaten not only because he couldn't help us
but also because he now realized that the war was not somewhere
far away, but right here. As we prepared to leave our host insisted
on providing us with food for the journey. When we reached the
train station, we saw long lines of freight trains filled with refugees
escaping deeper east into the depths of Russia. There was no question of buying tickets; it was chaos. Masses of people would gather

at the doors of the cattle cars and we had to use our elbows vigorously to secure a place that would let us reach the entrance of the wagon. I was able to jump in first and pull Shloime and Srulce into my wagon. Checking with the people inside our wagon, we were told that this train was headed to Stalingrad. That was fine with us; Stalingrad was quite far; we thought it unlikely that the enemy would reach there.

The trip took almost a week. The train would sometimes stop for hours at a time, and we never knew when it would start again. When the train stopped in a station people would jump off to get some "kipyatok" (boiling water); occasionally it was possible to purchase some food (bread, sour milk, cheese) from peasant women who stood near the "kipyatok" dispensers. There was plenty of time to think during the monotonous hours while the train raced eastward and we were being torn from our parents and sisters. Homesickness and regret gnawed at our hearts. Together we had at first escaped the clutches of the German army, and for what end? We had abandoned them. But the train moved further and further and the hope that we would ever see them again began to seem like a strained fantasy ... suddenly these thoughts were interrupted by the hooting whistle of the locomotive.

When we arrived near the main station in Stalingrad the

train stopped and the cattle doors were opened. Government functionaries greeted us with the announcement that we had to report to a particular government office to register and to be signed up for work. We were glad to hear it and moved briskly along with those who had already began to march. Arriving at the building which housed the office, we found that hundreds had preceded us. We had to join a long line to reach the officials who registered us and it took most of the rest of the day. When it became our turn with the official, he looked into our passports and noticed that there was a notation that we were refugees from Poland.

He told us that we couldn't remain in Stalingrad; he would send us to a "Kolhoz" (a communal farm). We wanted very much to be in one place so we wouldn't have to drag ourselves from one place to another one more time. I remember that before leaving for the Kolhoz we went to a restaurant nearby. We were struck by the notice on the door of the restaurant that they were offering ten different courses, all for one very reasonable price. We were, of course, curious to find out how they could offer such a generous selection for such reasonable cost. Of course, once we sat down, the mystery revealed itself; this is how they calculated: the soup was one course, the bread a second, a piece of meat was third, a few peas were fourth, a carrot was fifth, one potato was the sixth course, a piece of onion seventh, the "compot" was the eight course, a cookie nine, and the tea the tenth course. A sumptuous meal indeed – one doesn't forget such moments!

We were very tired and decided to go to the Kolhoz at once. The officials had given us directions how to get there. We had to go to the Volga River on the east side of Stalingrad and at a certain station on shore pick up a particular passenger steamer which would take us south. About two hours later we were to disembark at a small stop at which drovers with horse-drawn wagons from the Kolhoz were picking up provisions from the steamer. We were to hitch a ride with these drovers to the communal settlement. Walking to the wide river, we observed that Stalingrad was a very industrialized large city. There were factories with many chimneys spewing smoke. All we were interested in, however, was some rest; we had been on the run for almost nine days and were exhausted. Arriving at the shore station we ran up the plank to the first steamer that was going south, having explained to the shore official that we were refugees assigned to a particular Kolhoz. He seemed to know the procedure already and allowed us to board without tickets.

On board we observed our fellow passengers. They all seemed to be peasants with weather-beaten faces, the lines showing hard labour and poverty. Most were dressed in rags; quite a contrast from the people in Ukraine and especially Dniepropetrovsk were citizens seemed much more prosperous. After almost two hours steaming downstream, our stop was called out and we disembarked. Descending the gang plank we saw two wagons harnessed with oxen on the rise above the River's shore. Nothing else greeted us; there was no building, no trees, not even grass, only a bit of sand-blown steppe. We asked the drovers if they were from the Kolhoz we were assigned to reach and they answered affirmatively. We had arrived. After the drovers loaded the various bags and some barrels of oil for machinery onto the wagons, there was no room for us. One of the drovers began cursing, not un-humorously, in frustration and invited us somewhat sarcastically not to be lazy and to try and use our delicate city-bred feet as he, too, had no room on his wagon and we all would have to walk alongside. We had no choice; of course, it turned out the communal settlement was about 20 kilometres from the river, a good four hours. Some welcome!

All we saw on the walk was the sky, the scrubby earth and sand. Not a tree. When we finally stopped, what greeted us were four poles supporting some sort of roof, corrugated tin perhaps, without any walls. Under this roof there were some rows of wooden pallets and some field cots, most covered by gauze-like netting. We asked why there was netting and we were told that since the villagers slept over because it was too far to go home to the village, they needed the netting to protect them against the swarms of mosquitoes. We asked where we would sleep; the foreman tried to find a place for us but couldn't. He explained that he didn't expect us and therefore there was no preparation of a sleeping place for us. The best we could do was to bring some of the plentiful straw nearby and stretch out on the ground with whatever clothing we were wearing. Sleep was virtually impossible. Without netting we were bitten mercilessly by the hordes of mosquitoes and we prayed for morning to arrive.

Early in the morning one of the villagers indicated what kind of work we were expected to do. Because all the young men and the horses were mobilized by the military, only older men and women were left to work on the Kolhoz; they were, therefore, quite glad to have us to help. The foreman took me and led me to the oxen lying not far from the sleeping station. I would have to learn how to harness two oxen to a wagon. It turned out that only certain oxen could be paired. He pointed to one animal, and then to another about forty feet way and said: "this is your pair." To me they all looked alike, each reddish brown with large white spots. He showed me how to tell them apart and how to harness my couple. First I had to tie a special knot over the two horns and lead the first one – the more willing – to the other. Once that was accomplished I tied a similar knot on the partner. Once done I was able to lead them to the wagon, then carefully put a joint yoke over them. Once it was in place, I was able to slip the wooden axle from the wagon into the special stirrup hanging from the middle of the yoke between the two oxen.

This was not work for a tailor's apprentice, but eventually I got the hang of it. While driving them, you had to talk to the oxen; one of mine, on the right side was called "Tzop," and the one on the left was "Tzebe." It wasn't easy. However, remembering how the Germans had tortured us, this work was not so terrible, considering also that our Russian fellow workers had to do the same work. A few kilometres from the sleeping station a huge combine was harvesting wheat. Our job was to bring the wagons alongside and parallel to the combine on its right side, and moving slowly at the same speed, have the grain pipe fill our wagons with the wheat kernels. Then we would return to the sleeping station and on a flat area nearby we would dump the wheat by lifting the boards in the rear of the wagon. For the last part we had to get into the wagon and shovel the rest out. Back and forth, all day long, we moved between the combine and the sleeping station, till dusk. Sometime during the middle of the day we stopped to eat the inadequate piece of bread with water that was our lunch. Oxen have the occasional habit of becoming obstinate and refusing to move (that's why they're oxen). When you try to force them with blows to go on, they can suddenly start into a kind of awkward wild gallop and one of the wheels would drop off and they would finally stop. Fortunately, when it happened to me I was returning empty to the combine. Of course, chasing them was a special torture. The combine leaves a three or four inch stubble after cutting the wheat, and these bottom blades are sharp. By then I had already worn out my shoes and now had to chase the oxen barefoot over these sharp little stalks. It was like running on a bed of upturned nails – torture! After two weeks of walking on these fields the soles of my feet were like wooden boards.

At the same, we were being starved. They gave us some bread and a few pieces of salted dry fish. The other villagers brought some food from their homes. We could see that they too had very little; it was a very poor Kolhoz. Even though we were the only strangers in this Kolhoz, they sometimes shared what little food they had with us and this helped a little, but it was not enough. At night the mosquitoes continued their particular torture and even exhausted, we could hardly sleep. No one seemed to care about us. We were getting desperate and we knew we would not survive, so we began to consider escape. But how to do it? The Volga River was at least a four hour march away. Leaving was not a problem since we slept virtually in the open. We decided to wait till after receiving our weekly ration of bread. The following morning, before dawn, with our treasured loaf of bread wrapped in an old shirt, we slipped out of camp and began marching briskly back on the dry rutted road which had brought us from the river stop to this place. It was then the end of July and it was hot, even in the morning. With the Kolhoz far behind us, we marched towards an unknown destiny. But one reassuring thing we did know: we had bread for at least for four or five days. When I recall today those three weeks in the Kolhoz on the dry steppe, I'm convinced I could never have mastered the work with the oxen, nor endured running barefoot on the sharp stubbles left by the combine. We can only survive these experiences when there are no alternatives. But it does have some usefulness for the future. Still, quite early in the day we arrived at the river. The sun was shinning magnificently and was reflected on the flowing water. We sat down at the shore and waited for a steamer to arrive. One soon arrived and we crossed the plank to get on the boat. The ship cast off and we were once again going south with the current to the city of Astrakhan on the Caspian Sea.

CHAPTER 14

Charabali

It was early August; we sat on our bundles. The steamer was crowded, mainly with peasant women. We heard mostly Russian, but also other dialects. We ourselves drew attention. A Russian came near us and asked us where we're from. We told him that we were evacuated from the front areas and we were looking for work. Of course we didn't divulge that we'd just escaped from a Kolhoz. He told us in an authoritative tone that in "our" Russia there are no unemployed. Then he added that in about an hour on the way to Astrakhan the steamer would stop at a small station called Charabali where there was a large factory that made all kinds of conserves. He knew that they needed workers and assured us that in the complex there was a good restaurant and we wouldn't go hungry. He suggested that it would be easier for us in Charabali than in a big city like Astrakhan. Listening to him, we felt that he didn't have any ulterior motives and his advice made sense. In the conversation that followed, he revealed that he knew the factory very well because he had worked there in a supervisory capacity. Now he was being transferred to another location. We felt that he was trying genuinely to be helpful and we decided to disembark in Charabali (the name alone sounded so exotic). When the ship landed, a number of the passengers got off, as did we with our small bundles. We followed the others along a sandy dirt road towards the village with the exotic name. It was a hot, dry, desert-like day. The land in all directions was flat, with no trees in sight. After about a half an hours walk we reached the small outlying farm houses. The streets were not paved, not even with cobble-stones, and without sidewalks we saw only a few boards in front of the entrance to some of the houses. We asked for the administrative building in the village so we could register. The clerk, in military uniform (who we later realized was a police clerk), inquired where we were coming from. We told him we were coming from Stalingrad, having been evacuated from Sarny (in our passports there was a stamp that we had lived in Sarny). He asked some other questions but seemed quite sympathetic to us. He told us, yes, indeed, the factory needed workers. But before we could apply for work there we needed to have an address. He called in a helper from another room – a swarthy shorter man of about forty - and told us: "this man will take you where you can settle in; tomorrow you'll go to the factory, which is only about two kilometres from here, and apply for work." He gave us a hand-scribbled note to the director of the factory and we went off with the other fellow.

The swarthy man who led us off was actually a tartar, and a very fine fellow. He took us to a side street and to a small hut-like house which contained two rooms and a kitchen. Of course, it looked very abandoned, but to us it appeared like a palace. We had a place! And tomorrow we knew we were going to get work. The man brought us some cots to sleep on. After such a long day, having escaped so early in the morning from the Kolhoz, and in the same day finding a place to sleep like human beings knowing that the mosquitoes would not eat us up, we soon fell into a deep, satisfying sleep. We woke early, had breakfast of some bread from the cache we had taken with us, with some water, and went off briskly to the factory. After a half hour walk we saw a complex, mostly of single floor buildings dominated by a high chimney, surrounded by a high fence of bricks and wire. There was a main gate with a guard to whom we showed our note from the police clerk in the village. He let us in and we inquired where the office of the director was.

We found the director, a tall, handsome young man in his middle thirties, dressed in a suit. We showed him our note and after a few questions he called someone from the back office to register us and then to take us to our jobs. The man took us outside to a courtyard where six or seven horse-drawn wagons heaped high with boxes of vegetables, tomatoes and fruit, like plums, apples, and pears were arriving. The drovers were unloading the wagons and my brother and I were told to help them. My brother-in-law was taken to another part of the factory. Once the wagons were emptied we were told to drive with the drovers to a railway siding about half a kilometre away. A freight train had arrived full of vegetables and fruit and we had to load the wagons to transfer the goods to the factory where we unloaded them again. While unloading we were allowed to eat the fruit, but taking any with us was strictly forbidden. Punctually at 12:30 we stopped for lunch; we were taken to a modern cafeteria in the factory where we could buy a generous meal quite reasonably priced. My brother-in-law joined us. For the first time in weeks we had a proper, tasty hot meal. After two days my brother was also transferred to another part of the factory.

A few days later, once the train had been emptied and we were awaiting the next one, the foreman called me aside and asked if I was willing to drive my own horse and wagon. I said yes and he asked, "you think you can handle a horse?" I answered that a man who was willing could learn anything, and I was willing. The fact is, it was a little easier if you were a driver because there were occasional minutes to yourself even though you had to do your own loading and unloading. He liked my answer and the next day I had my own horse and wagon. Next morning early, I showed up at the horse barn where about 40 horses were stabled. There I found the overseer of the horses; he knew already that I had been assigned to the wagons and expected me. He too asked me whether I had handled horses and I answered, no, but I had handled oxen. He started laughing; "nu, ladno, uvidim" (Nu, good, we shall see). He took me to one of the horses, a very tall one, brown with a white mark on the forehead between the eyes. The overseer told me that the other drovers avoided this horses because it was quite "ornery." After work they would unharness the horses and ride them over to a small river nearby to have them drink; then they would ride them back. But this one, he told me, would not let himself be ridden. He also told me that I couldn't use a whip on this horse because it would make him wild and this was dangerous.

"Are you willing to work with this one?" he asked. I was too proud to refuse. He knew I was a Jew and I didn't want him to think Jews are cowards. I told him I was willing if he would show me how to put the bridle on and how to harness the horse to the wagon and all the other things one needed to know when working with the horses. "Nu, good, good," and he showed me how to approach the horse, always from the left side. Then he taught me the whole psychology of working with horses. Together we opened the horse's mouth to insert the bit while putting on the bridle. As it turned out, he was right in teaching me that a horse is an animal with feelings and will cooperate and be loyal to its master if he's considerate and gentle. I learned this fact more than once. The overseer taught how to be a good drover. The main thing he stressed was to be quiet and confident because the horse can feel it if the master isn't. I was a good pupil and became a real drover. I soon became good friends with my horse. Six thirty in the morning when I would walk into the barn he could already feel my presence in spite of the fact that it was still dark and his stall was about sixty feet from the entrance. He would greet me with a friendly "neigh" and when I stroked his shiny neck and his head, he would turn to try to reach my face as if to give it a kiss. It was almost as if he was trying to tell me something but didn't have the language.

I have to admit that I loved that animal, and even today, sixty years later, I still feel a bond to my "Chestnut," the name he was known by. I never had occasion to use the whip with him; he obeyed without any threat. Only once did we have a "fight" about who would be the victor. After each day of heavy work in the heat, unloading our fruit boxes or heavy bags of sugar at the factory, then returning to the train to load the wagon again for a second trip back to the factory, we couldn't wait for the day to end to unharness the horses and go to the river for the horses to drink. It was a few moments to relax and to exchange a few words with the other drovers. But I had a problem; the other drovers, healthy peasants from the area, were able to ride to the river and back after unharnessing their horses in the horse barn. I had to walk my 'Chestnut".

By the time I arrived at the river, the others were already preparing to return, and sometimes they made fun of me, in a friendly tone, that I was stuck with a horse that couldn't be ridden, and certainly not by a Jewish city boy. I heard this more than once. Once, while taking my horse to the river, I talked to the horse as much as to myself. "No, I'm not going to walk the horse to the river anymore. I have to ride like the others." And I remembered how when I was a small boy in Lomza, and riding a horse back for our milkman from the fields, some Polish boys whipped the horse and frightened him into a wild gallop with me clinging for life to the horse's mane. And I didn't fall off. ·

Was I to be afraid of a horse now, a strong, healthy young

man? No, no, I'll show them what a Jewish city-boy is capable of. I let "Chestnut" drink his fill at the river, then I walked him over to a large rock nearby. I got on the rock with my horse close by. With a sudden jump I was on his back, grabbing his mane and lying forward on his neck as close as possible. We were glued to each other. There was a split second of complete silence and then "Chestnut" began to neigh wildly and got high on his hind legs to throw me off. When that didn't work he began kicking high with his hind legs; then, jumping wildly, he circled again and again trying to shake me off. Although I was getting dizzy I didn't give up my hold and retained my alertness. I was aware that all the other drovers were watching this struggle between a man and a horse. After about ten minutes, the horse stopped its effort to unseat me and began walking slower and slower. I had won; from then on I had no trouble mounting him whenever I took him to the river to drink. My stature among the drovers had risen substantially; I heard no more jokes at the expense of Jews.

A few words about the factory. According to what I learned, the factory had been built by American engineers in 1936. All the machinery was from the U.S. It was almost fully automatic, but because it was such a large factory there were many people working there, mostly women. The drovers were all men because it was back-breaking work. Occasionally I had to unload bags of sugar that were 100 kilos, about 230 pounds. By then, my brother Shloime had stopped working at the factory. He had found a position in Charabali in a tailoring factory which filled government contracts. It paid better than the factory, but more important, there were all kinds of opportunities to earn extra outside of the system so that you could have money to buy goods on the black market. My brother-in-law Srulce was especially adept at bringing various conserves that didn't spoil so that we had enough to eat, and that was crucial. That was life in Russia. In other countries it was believed that everyone was equal in the Soviet Union; in actuality this was a fiction. Because of massive Russian propaganda, it was believed that because it was a socialist system, which preached equality for every one, it was really so. This was perhaps the greatest bluff of the 20th century.

Private business didn't exist; it was forbidden. Thus every worker was employed by the state. But the wages were very low so that no one could survive on them. Everyone had to find some way to increase his income; one had to do something that wasn't allowed in order to exist. In Russia there was a saying. "There are three categories of citizens: those that had been in prison, those who are presently incarcerated, and those who will be in prison."

Understandably, there was a "black market" where the prices were twenty or thirty times higher than government prices. Government prices were, indeed, cheap, but unfortunately there were no products for sale. The privileged officials of the Communist Party had special stores stocked with all kinds of goods available to them at government prices. So this was the "equality" that existed in this socialist "heaven." There was no private initiative. For instance, if there was a surplus of something in one area and someone tried to sell to an area that had a shortage of this product, he would automatically be sentenced for a crime against the state as a speculator. The lack of private initiative created hardship for the people and led to great corruption in the society.

One day I brought sacks with hard sugar from the train to the factory. When I was on my last sack, a lady, a foreman, told me to empty it into a crate. When I had shaken out the last of the sugar into the crate, I took three small pieces and put them into the pockets of my apron. As I turned to leave, the same woman approached and asked what I had in my pocket. I took out the three pieces of sugar and she asked me for my name. Coming to work the next morning, my foreman told me that I have to go to the office of the Director (I had already forgotten about the previous day). Approaching the building which housed the Director's office, I noticed on the wall a large poster which declared: "Michael Abramovitch Gruda, a worker in our plant, has committed a crime by stealing from the state." I remember there was more, all in large letters, which I don't remember. A veil of fear descended on me as I read this proclamation. I went into the Director's office to report. He took a while to look at me, and then proceeded to give me a lecture. "Thieving from our socialist state! Here we sit in jail for stealing; there they will teach you what it means to steal from your government." He went on in this manner. When I had a chance to speak, I told him everything about myself and begged him to forgive this one instance. I told him that now I know how to appreciate the Soviet homeland, and I will conduct myself so as to be a model for others. After a moment of thought he took a piece of stationary and wrote out a note to my foreman to let me continue to work (later I found out that the young, handsome Director was a Jew).

In Charabali there was a movie theatre where they showed news clips of the War. In spite of the heroic language of the commentators, it was clear that Russian forces were retreating across the whole front. There was also an influx of refugees to Charabali. One day the elderly tartar who led us to the house came to visit and told us that we three have to move into one room because another family of four was moving in. The family that arrived were Jewish, from Berditchev, with a fourteen year old son and a seventeen year old daughter. Their name was Kamenetsky. The father had been a lower city official, a simple, unassuming man, and we all got along well together. In time, we told them where we came from and how we left our family behind and that we didn't know how they were faring. I wonder if we thought that the high holidays might be getting close. I don't think so; we had lost track of time. There were no Jews in Charabali and the Kamenetskys were assimilated. My interest naturally drifted towards Donia, a pretty, sympathetic girl. I was just twenty-one and she was seventeen, a perfect match. We occasionally went walking together and once or twice went swimming in the little river nearby where I used to take the horses to drink. However, I was preoccupied with our situation and worry about our family, and she seemed very young and too naïve for me.

Soon the weather started changing. There were stronger winds, dry, but colder. Fall was coming, with winter not far behind. At the start of 1942, the situation at the front became terrible. The Russian army had suffered severely. The authorities were mobilizing more and more men. I received my draft notice at the end of January. The winter was severe and was beginning to take its

toll. In two weeks I was to report to the military offices in Charabali and I got ready to part from my brother and my brother-in-
law. In anticipation that my brother would also soon be drafted,
we agreed that we would both try to maintain contact with Srulce
in Charabali as he was in his late thirties and probably wouldn't be
drafted for quite a while. During this time I was friendly with Donia and told her about my family. It may sound strange, but parting with my horse was an emotional experience; even now I feel a
tug at my heart remembering and it is hard to put into words what
I felt; he was my friend and that's why I'm nostalgic even now. I
said goodbye to the Kamenetsky family and almost silently to my
brother and brother-in-law. Then I marched off to my designated
meeting point in Charabali.

Father, Mother, Rachel Gitl, Luba, Itche Nussen, Schloime, Moishe (Baby)
Rozhan, 1920

Itche Nussen with wife Sarah
Lomzha, Poland, 1940

Father, Sister Esther & Niece
Azerbajan, 1942

Moishe, Esther, Father, Shaia
Kotovsk, Russia, 1944

DP Camp
Poking, Germany, 1946

Moishe Gruda, and brother Schloime
Kotovsk, Russia, 1944

Moishe, Mania(Wife), Esther, Shaia
Poking, Germany, 1947

CHAPTER 15

Astrakhan

As I approached the military station in Charabali, a small flat building of cinder block, I noticed that I had been preceded by a group of about twenty young men, all clutching their little bundles of possessions, probably a little bread with perhaps a shirt and maybe an undershirt, not much more than a few rags. A uniformed officer, possibly a lieutenant, came out with a list and began to call out the names he had.

When he finished he had us line up in twos, told us that he was taking us to Astrakhan where we would be assigned to our units, and then marched us off to the tiny railway station half a kilometre away. From Charabali to Astrakhan is about four hours by train. We sat in the freight train on the floor and the four hours didn't seem too long. By about 1 in the afternoon we had arrived. The boys got acquainted during the trip. Most were from the area around Charabali and a few refugees, but I was the only Jew. The train stopped a little before the town and our lieutenant told us to get into formation and marched us to the Volga River about a forty minute walk away. Near the river where we arrived there was a small compound with about six buildings. He turned us over to another officer and then left. The new man assigned us to one of the buildings in which there were a number of rooms but no furniture. He told us we would sleep the night here on the floor. In spite of the cold and no heating in the building I managed to sleep through the night in my thick "Kufaika" (a heavy coat with its square patches filled with cotton batting).

Early in the morning they assembled us near the water and told us to wash. There was ice at the shore of the river; the Volga was solidly frozen. I remember that I had placed my little tin cup on the ice for a minute. Suddenly a gust of wind blew away my cup and I lost it. This was no small matter as it was hard to replace; in fact, losing any utensil was serious. Such goods were not available. Our short ablutions done, we received our "Payok," our rations. Each man got a large slice of bread and a little aluminum pot of barley soup. I could see that this was not enough to quench my hunger, but I had brought with me a sack of dried bread and packets of a mixture of conserved millet and barley, and kasha, already with some kind of fat in it, that only required heating in water, so I was able to stave off hunger.

After this "breakfast," a major appeared and gave us a patriotic lecture on our mission to defeat the German aggressors. Our battalion was a working battalion and our job was to build a new railway line from Astrakhan southeast to Kizlar in Georgia. We were a few hundred men and they divided us into smaller units. I remember that our first job was to lay track across the frozen Volga and slowly push empty freight cars along this track to the eastern shore of the river. The problem was that the retreat from the Germans was bringing vast numbers of trains with people and equipment from the Caucasus; the freight cars would be emptied and the locomotives would go back to evacuate more trains. Now the need was to get these wagons across the Volga and keep them out of German hands. At the same time the Russians were rushing to build the railway tracks south to Georgia and these empty freight cars would become trains on the new railway line.

After a week we were assigned to a digging detail. I saw, however, that the situation was not getting better. We were still sleeping in our clothing in the same cold building, the sanitary conditions were abysmal, and, the main thing, we were not getting enough to eat. My own supplies were dwindling. At the same time I noted that the officers were getting more food and other privileges. One day they called us outside in groups of about fifty or sixty.

The commander asked each of us how much schooling we had. When I told him that I had finished seventh grade, he announced that I was now the commander of my own group of about twenty men. It is necessary to explain something: all those who were mobilized into the working battalions were in some way lacking in the eyes of the regime. The battalion consisted of people who had been released from jail, or other institutions, people whom the regime did not trust. As well, there were men from conquered territories, "freed people," and Poles who – like myself – were from territories under German control. These were our faults. Also, many of the men were illiterate. In other words, being made commander of this kind of a bunch was no great privilege or honour. My job was to make sure that they worked, fulfilled their tasks, and to report to my superior. My main task was to serve as an example of how hard they should work. The commander of our battalion was a major, probably from the NKVD, the secret police. We learned that the plan was to build the new railway line from Astrakhan to Kizlar, a dream from the time of the Tsars but not possible because of a lack of resources. Now, when they were able to mobilize over 100,000 men for the task, they were able to realize the project, to connect Georgia to Astrakhan so as not to have to go in a roundabout way that would expose them to the advancing Germans. This was a very important project, and the railway authorities wanted to have it under their control. But we had military status as if we were mobilized into the army. Eventually the railway bosses won and asserted their control over us even though we had military status.

A few days later we were told that we would be living in the freight cars, and they prepared stacked plank cots around the wall of the wagons. Accidentally I heard rumours that the leadership was trying to find trades people to serve the workers on the railway. I also heard that they were trying to establish tailoring to patch the torn clothing of the workers. When I approached the leadership about this rumour and told them that I was a tailor, they told me "no, you're not; you are a commander, and commanders are not recruited for tailoring." Now I realized that I had to get rid of this "promotion."I still possessed a few packs of tobacco, which was like having a fortune. I approached my own commander and told him quite openly that I had a pack of tobacco and he could have it if he demoted me.

There were three Jewish fellows who were tailors. Our commander informed us that in a few days we would leave on a special mission, and there we would see how to organize a tailoring group for the workers. And, indeed, a few days later we left in our train. After a night of travel we came out of our wagons in the morning, but we didn't know where we were. We were about 400 men divided into units made up of those in a wagon, with an "elder" in charge of each wagon. We were told that we were in a region called Baskumchak, not far from Stalingrad, with a village and a small lake by the same name. In this area there were stone quarries, and we were to load special wagons with these stones from the quarries to be used to secure the railway tracks. Sometimes they woke us at 2 am in the night when the stone trains would arrive; they were not to be kept waiting. We had to load the stones immediately. We were provided with canvas gloves because the recently dynamited stones were as sharp as knives, but after an hour or so they would tear and we ended up with bloodied hands. Later we found out that this work had previously been done by prisoners sentenced for heavy crimes. However, they had evacuated these prisoners deeper into Russia, so now we took over. In the morning we would be fed a watery soup with a bit of floating kasha. My personal supply of food had been used up.

People in my wagon were beginning to have scurvy, and some were beginning to lose their teeth. Some became so weak that they couldn't go to work. They were taken away and vanished. One of the boys I had befriended had been a student from a well-to-do family from Lvov. He couldn't adjust to the hard work and was one of the first to succumb. The nights were bitterly cold in the unheated wagons and we were tortured by dreams of bread. For almost two months we continued, those of us who survived. Once while standing in line to receive chits for the noon meal, I noticed an attractive, neatly dressed woman almost in middle age giving them out. When I reached her she gave me two. When I pointed it out to her, she said it's alright. She asked me where I was from; I told her in a few sentences and mentioned that I was a tailor. From then on she became very interested in me and helped me to get more to eat. She herself, she told me, was from Astrakhan and her husband was a major in the army. She had volunteered for the work here. Since the leadership of the camp had their own, more comfortable, wagons and she lived in one of them she was privy to all kinds of information not known to us. Once, she told me that a special wagon was to arrive in a few days that had built-in show-ers. We hadn't showered for more than five weeks and we were pestered by lice. She also told me that in a week or so we would be shipped back to Astrakhan and I would be free of this work and the terrible conditions we had endured.

It was the best news I had had in many months. She told me that she had spoken to the responsible leadership about creating a tailoring service to mend the workers' clothing. We were walking around virtually in torn rags. I will never forget this woman; she helped me like an angel in the worst times I was to experience during all my time in Russia. Till today I'm not clear why she undertook to help me; perhaps I was too young and naïve to realize that she was attracted to me.

CHAPTER 16

Back To Astrakhan

One night, while the encampment was sleeping, our train began to move. As we learned later, we were going south to Astrakhan. About five or six hours later, in the morning, we arrived outside of Astrachan not far from the Volga. The land was flat, and because the spring thaw had set in, the Volga flooded the area. Even though we had stopped on a slight rise above the plain, the water reached virtually to the floors of our wagons. It was as if we were in the middle of a lake and around us were floating thousands and thousands of 8"x 10"x 8' wooden rails for the train tracks. The wooden rails had been treated with tar, and because getting from one wagon to the next required getting into the water and holding on to the wooden rails, our hands were full of the tar that was beginning to melt in the hot spring sun. Needless to say, the tar soon found its way to our faces and we began to look like commandos in blackface. Of course, we had no soap to wash off the tar and the heat from the sun made the tar on our faces burn our skin, an extremely painful sensation that only eased at night. We tried during the day to get some of the tar off by using sand to rub it from our faces.

Because of the flooding we couldn't work and had an unexpected rest. Soon after arriving, I noticed a little boat floating a few hundred meters away. No one seemed to be in it. Using one of the wooden rails I swam over and was pleased to see that there was one oar in the boat. I slowly pulled myself into the boat at the back so as not to turn it over. Once inside I was able to paddle slowly - canoe style – by sitting backwards at the pointy front of the little boat. After about two kilometres I noticed some peasant houses on the shore and headed towards them. The peasants greeted me cordially and I told them where I had come from. They told me that the flood was preventing them from selling some of their private produce and they were happy to sell me some. I bought cheese, milk and yoghurt and headed back. You can imagine how happy my friends in our wagon were to share in this bounty. We were still being fed too little and I had lost my generous lady mentor, although she had given me her address in Astrakhan. Three times in the next ten days I repeated my trip to the peasants. I had stored the boat among an especially dense grouping of rails near the shore. Once in swimming towards the boat, the slippery rail under my right arm suddenly turned over and I lost my hold on it. Down I went into what seemed an endless hole underneath the water. I was not a very good swimmer yet, and for an instant I panicked and swallowed a lot of water, thinking that, for sure this was my end. But I was lucky and managed to get to the surface and then suddenly felt ground under my feet. I reached the shore and carefully made my way to the boat to continue my "shopping" trip.

Then the flooding receded and we had to begin to work. I, however, had a lucky break. The commander of the whole encampment called me in and told me, "Misha – (short for Michael) – Abramovich, we are going to make a tailoring shop and you will have a wagon to fix the men's clothing."

Eventually we did get a separate wagon where I and some of the other men who had tailoring experience began to fix the tattered clothing. It's hard to explain how we managed to get needles and thread; at the time we had no sewing machine and had to repair old clothing with old rags using only needles and thread. I had become friendly with the commander and explained to him that if we could find a sewing machine somewhere, we could do more and much finer work, not only patches. After a while I had a chance to explain to him that I had been mobilized in Charabali, which I considered my home and where I still had my brother-in-law. I asked him if I could have permission to go back for three days; it was only three or four hours from where we were and on the spur line that we were working on. He felt kindly towards me and gave me permission to go and gave me a pass for a two day leave.

I had no problem now reaching Charabali. We were on the only line going north, and all I had to do was to note a freight train going north. I could then jump on the little steps at the end of the last wagon and I would get closer to Charabali. It sounds easy described this way, but it's not so simple. Throughout my years in Russia during those chaotic times, riding the rails was not an infrequent necessity for me and I became quite adept at it. Even as a teenager in Rozhan I was active in all kinds of sports and I especially excelled in the high and long jump. Living in the wagon as I was, jumping off and on the wagon was a daily necessity. One gets used to everything. People had already explained to me that jumping on and off trains needed a special approach to reduce the danger. Besides that, one has to be determined, focused, healthy and strong. I was all of twenty two during the summer of 1942; these were years when nothing seemed too difficult for me, so I was ready and eager to ride the rails to Charabali.

Not far from our wagons there was a freight train of about

40 wagons getting ready to leave and I noticed that a locomotive was being connected to the front end. It was a sign that the train was going to head north. To get on immediately was not a good idea because I would get caught; the train had to be moving well already. I ran alongside faster than the train was moving. Once it had reached about twenty kilometres an hour I waited for the last wagon and grabbing the railing at the back steps, hoisted myself on board. This had to be done rapidly but I had no difficulty. The train picked up speed, perhaps sixty to seventy kilometres an hour. As I knew the names of the stations we were passing, I had a good idea of approximately when we would be arriving in Charabali. I noticed that in passing small stations the train sped through, but in larger stations it slowed down while passing. Soon I stood on the back steps; more than two hours had gone by and I estimated that in about ten minutes we would be approaching Charabali. The moment came and a decision had to be made; if I didn't jump the train would take me past the town and I would end somewhere far away. To jump from the train one has to jump in the same direction as the train is moving, but you hit the ground with impact.

With all my force I jumped forward parallel with the moving train and in a split second I was rolling down the incline from the rails. I got up to see where I was and I saw the station not far from where I had landed. I began to walk to the house where we lived. Arriving, I knocked on the door; I didn't expect the men to be there as they were likely at work, but I hoped Mrs. Kamenetsky would be at home. Sure enough, she opened the door; a look of surprise crossed her face, but it changed to happiness. "Moishe," she exclaimed. I told her that I was on two days leave. I also told her what had happened to me and where I was stationed. I walked in and went to the room I had shared with my brother and brother-in-law, I now felt the weariness and the ache from the jump I had ignored in the excitement of coming. I lay down on one of the beds and rested but couldn't fall asleep from the excitement.

Some hours later, in the evening, my brother-in-law returned from work and was delighted to see me. I told him everything I had experienced. He in turn was able to give me my brother's address; my brother had been mobilized shortly after I had left, but he was in a regular army unit, not a work brigade. We spent the evening after supper talking about the War and about the Germans still victorious, even approaching Stalingrad. We commiserated about our family that had been left in Sarny, now under German occupation. We feared for my parents, my sisters, including his wife and his little daughter Luba. While we were talking, the Kamenetskys' daughter Donia listened very attentively and occasionally asked questions. Srulce had accumulated a respectable supply of preserves and now insisted that I take a good part back with me when I returned. The next day, after Srulce went to work and after I had said goodbye to him and the Kamenetskys, I took a sack full of preserves and walked to the station. I had to make sure to be back on time so as not be designated a deserter. When I arrived at the little building that was the Charabali train station, I noticed a military guard walking back and forth. He was alone on the platform. I realized I had to explain.

I approached him and explained that I had worked here and that I had been mobilized from here; now I had to return to my unit after visiting my relatives. I showed my leave pass and asked him how I could get back on a train. Of course, I knew what to do, but if I "enlisted" him in my effort, he wouldn't get suspicious and arrest me for jumping on the train, something strictly forbidden. He saw I was sincere and advised me to sit down, wait for one of the trains that stopped at Charabali, and get on it only after it had started moving; at that point he would look away and pretend not to see me getting on. That's what I did; after a few freight trains that sped by, one finally stopped, and after a few minutes began moving slowly again. I got on without any incident and three hours later was once more in Astrakhan, but with a sack full of food. Now I only had to worry that the food wouldn't be stolen from me.

The tailors and shoemakers had been given a separate wagon for our work; and we lived there too. We were three shoemakers, three tailors, and a barber. The shoemakers were Russian, the tailors Jews, as was the barber, a man from Stanislavov, Galicia. One day a young fellow arrived carrying a large portable sewing machine, we were never able to find out from where and how he had acquired it. His name was David Israelit and he hailed from Dvinsk, Latvia; when he spoke Yiddish it was hard to understand him because he spoke with a lisp, and especially had difficulty pronouncing the "sh" sound which came from him as a thin "ccc." He was a very enterprising fellow, but not much of a tailor. He struck a bargain with me that I should take him in as a tailor and he would share his sewing machine with us; we would also share any earnings to be had. I was happy to agree; we had been working only with needles and now we could produce faster. Young as he was, David was very stingy; we used to kid him about it and he would answer "I have a saying; "as men cist (for shist) bin Ich nit do, un as men tzailt gelt bin Ich do (when they shoot I'm not here, but when they count money I'm there)."

The Germans were coming closer and closer to Stalingrad.

The situation was worsening. German bombers were bombing us almost every night, always at midnight; why midnight, we couldn't tell. Trains are always a target in wartime. When we heard the planes we would get out of the wagons and run off into the fields. The impact of the bombs, even when they didn't hit a wagon – and they didn't often – shook the ground so strongly that they derailed the wagons. In the morning we had to work hard manually to put them back on the rails. True to his own saying, David was terrified of the bombing. Every time we were bombed our young "tailor" used to literally shit in his pants. One of the other tailors, Shaya Farbiasz from the Lublin area, eventually became part of my family.

CHAPTER 17

Lineynoe

It was Winter of 1942 and the battles around Stalingrad were gruesome. There was talk that we might have to evacuate deeper into Russia. Just the suggestion of this made us depressed. Some young Jewish fellows exclaimed that they would not evacuate; they'd had enough of running away. I told them that they were crazy; under no circumstances would I take the chance to fall under the Germans occupation again.

Indeed, the situation was very tense: there was constant movement of full troop trains moving towards the front. Our commanders told us that shortly we would also be moved closer to Stalingrad. Some days later, as we slept, we felt the train we were living in moving. At dawn our train stopped and then a little later it moved again. Because it was dark we couldn't make out where we were and then a little later it moved again. When it became light we stopped and we could see that we had been shunted to a dead end track away from the main lines. We could see hard, sandy soil in all directions. Far in the distance we could see small houses. Our commanders told us that we had arrived; here we would secure the rail lines.

Before we had left Astrakhan, they had sent us about ten men to board in our wagon. Among them were not only political prisoners but also plain criminals. They had mobilized them for the defence of Stalingrad. Just to hear their foul language with its Russian unprintable swearwords was dizzying. These were our new "neighbours." In the early hours they would leave to work with the others on the rail lines, but when they returned in the evening it became lively in our wagon. They were a noisy bunch, and when we retired to sleep, they would help themselves to our food without bothering to ask permission. The situation became unbearable. We could not complain to our commander because we knew that he himself was afraid of them. The best solution, we agreed, was to speak to them ourselves. As the man responsible for our tailoring operation, it fell to me to make the attempt. At the first opportunity, I began a conversation with the one who was the leader, a man even his comrades were afraid of, a big muscular brute of a man. We were sitting alone at the entrance of the freight car, our legs dangling over the edge. I still remember his name, Kondratiev. I told him about my self and then invited him to do likewise about himself. For a moment the War seemed far away. He looked at me with some surprise, then replied slowly almost with tenderness: "Oy, 'Malcik, Malcik (little fellow), this I can't tell you; but I promise you, no one will touch your things anymore." We looked at each other and for a moment I thought his eyes were moist, as were mine from the recollection of what I had gone through. Then he added, "ladno, ladno (good, good)." A few moments later he turned in the direction of his comrades and loudly proclaimed: "No one, no one better dare get close to their possessions. Is it clear? I'll say no more." We, of course, came to thank him with little favours that he came to appreciate.

There were days when we would not receive our "payok," our rations for the day. There were many reasons for it. Some nights we lay on our planks and couldn't fall asleep because of gnawing hunger; other nights we would suddenly wake up to the thunder of German bombs exploding on the rail lines and the stationary or moving trains nearby. Then we would hear the reassuring cannonades of the responding anti-aircraft guns. When things quieted down afterwards, one of the men in our wagon, Shurupov, a former principal of a higher educational institution (he had probably sinned politically and so was incarcerated with the actual criminals) began to tell us folk tales. He was a wonderful raconteur and to this day I remember vividly some of his stories.

I remember the many Uzbeks who died. They were brought to work on the railways, but the lack of adequate food did them in. Perhaps they were also susceptible to disease and, of course, their inability to speak Russian didn't help them.

One day we were visited by the commanding officer of the entire operation. Colonel Kostenko, a tall, handsome man, told us that it had been decided that the tailoring, shoemaking, and barbering operation was to be transferred from the wagon to the nearest village from where we would service the entire battalion. The village was the one we had first seen in the distance. This was Lineynoe.

For us this was the best news. The day arrived when we were finally told to leave our wagon. The commanders didn't provide any transportation to the village, about 3 or 4 kilometres away; all horses, of course, had been mobilized. There wasn't even a road, but we could follow a rough pathway between the shrubs. The soil was mostly sandy, and it was difficult to walk in this shifting sand. We had to carry the sewing machine on our backs, so we alternated every few hundred meters. One commander had told us how to find the hut in the village that we would be occupying. As we approached the village we began to pass little huts. No one seemed to be around. We had been given a number for the hut we were to enter. It was on the second side street near the corner; of course the streets were not paved, but since it was not the rainy season, the few streets were not muddy.

Entering the hut, we found one large room which our group made up of three tailors, two shoemakers, and the barber had to work in and also use as living quarters. Still, compared with the wagon we had left, it was palatial, especially without the rough neighbours we had had to endure. The village was very poor and the people were all Tartars; the able bodied men had all been mobilized. Early in the morning all the women went to a kolhoz not far away. Returning in the evening, they were too exhausted to converse and in any case they didn't speak Russian. Not only were we not able to buy any food from them, but they had hoped that we would give them some. To obtain our food, we sent a young fellow to the cooking wagon to fetch our daily soup and bread. Although he knew nothing of the trade, we had gotten him as a fourth tailor, for the express purpose of fetching our daily food. Unfortunately, on the way back he would help himself to the kasha, or occasionally noodles, at the bottom of the pail. By the time the soup reached us there was not enough solid nourishment for the rest of us. We warned him not to repeat this, but he couldn't help himself and continued so we had to let him go. Our situation was not sustainable; we had to find a source of additional food.

One day, I suddenly had a strong headache and a high fever; I was shivering even though it was quite warm outside. No matter how much I covered myself with whatever I had, I still shivered from cold and had convulsions. I couldn't sleep and was plagued by indescribable nightmares and hallucinations. My co-workers sent for the doctor serving the train workers. After examining me, he gave me the good news: I had malaria and unfortunately he had no medicine. He promised to try and get some quinine for me and explained what I could expect. The high fever and shivering attacks came at the same time each day. I lost a lot of weight and became quite thin. I simply couldn't eat any food. On the fourth day the doctor brought me a little quinine, a very bitter medicine. He brought the powder in a piece of paper, and I had to transfer it to a smaller, thinner piece of newspaper – probably "Pravda" – to swallow. One couldn't swallow the quinine directly, it was so bitter. Unfortunately I didn't have enough of the medicine, so the attacks went on for more than three weeks. Then they stopped; but at the end of two weeks they started once more, again for three or four days. This pattern continued every two weeks for another six months. Interestingly, they always came back at the same time and for the same length. I know there were a lot of people dying of malaria; I was one of the few lucky ones to survive. Slowly, I overcame my malady, but I still suffered a return of these attacks once or twice a year; doctors told me that it would continue returning for a long time, but fortunately after ten years it finally left me alone.

Finally we had good news. A whole German army was trapped in and around Stalingrad. Although there were fierce battles, we felt that this was a breakthrough that would eventually lead to victory. Our situation, however, was still not very good because we didn't have enough to eat. Everything was being sent to the front which had obvious priority.

One day the Commanding Officer, Kostenko, came to our hut and told us the following: a whole regiment was coming to the village to rest from the battles around Stalingrad. At the same time both official newspapers, "Izvestia" and "Pravda," announced that all Russian officers would be issued military jackets, like officers of other armies. Till now officers wore long shirts similar to those of soldiers over their slacks, belted by a special cross belt with a pistol on the hip. Officer insignia was visible on the shirt collar because there were no epaulets on their shirts. Kostenko asked me if we would be able to make the new officer jackets and the long officer coats with wide lapels and epaulets. And then he added: if we could accomplish this, then he would be able to fulfil his assignment. Since I had a good relationship with him, I asked what had his assignment got to do with the new uniforms. He responded with a lecture on the way Soviet industry worked that I never forgot. He said that the regiment that was arriving had a lot of trucks which he needed desperately to accomplish his assignment with the trains on time. He added that when he discussed the news about the new uniforms with the army officers they were extremely excited. He suddenly realized that he could tell the officers that he had good tailors who would be able to make their new uniforms. "Now it's up to you. Can you undertake to make these new uniforms?" We had seen photographs of the models of these new uniforms on a whole page of the newspapers, and I could assure him that we would be pleased to make the new uniforms.

Kostenko was extremely pleased and ordered us not to take on any more work from the train workers because from now on we were to be attached to the regiment that was arriving, and we would be getting the same rations that the regiment was providing while we would continue to receive the food coming to us from the train kitchen, but in dry form.

I received a list of all the officers for whom we would be sewing the new uniforms. At the top of the list were the colonels and then the majors. They received the material and they brought it to us. Each one promised that I would receive additional rewards if I completed his uniform ahead of his place on the list. A source of all kinds of good things opened for us. We received flour, tobacco – which was like getting diamonds – potatoes, jams, even wine and liquor, and tangerines. Each senior officer had a way of acquiring these delicacies. When we began making the officers' uniforms, we requested of our commanders that the shoemakers and the barber be moved from our room. For three months we had plenty of everything we wanted. As I was still recovering from my malaria, this plenty contributed to my recovery. A group of Jewish boys working hard on the rails nearby would come to our room in the evenings and we supplied them with food.

I then became an expert cook for the group as the responsibility somehow devolved on me when I had mentioned that I knew how. My specialty was Ukrainian borsht, sometimes including gazelle meat hunted by some of the officers. The mud oven we used was in the middle of the room and to heat it we had to go into the field to harvest a heavy, thick type of straw six feet high called "kashmish," probably a tartar word, which burned well and very quickly. The main thing was that we had good food, and plenty of it. This was the bitterest time of the war in Russia, when a tiny container of tobacco, called "mahorka," fetched 700 rubles. One potato could cost 5 rubles, when an ordinary labourer's wages might be 150 rubles a month. In most factories a worker could buy something to eat more cheaply at the cafeteria, but he could not extend this to his family. The result was that everybody had to steal when possible. We, however, had a whole suitcase of tobacco and delicacies, and a whole sack of potatoes.

However, everything comes to an end, especially in wartime. The regiment which had become the reason for our prosperity had to leave for the front after three months. Our Commander, Kostenko, was pleased with his idea of having traded our tailoring services for additional trucks from this regiment. With these additional trucks he was able to fulfil his assignment. My relationship with him became much closer and he confided in me that very soon we would be leaving this place, Lineynoe. After the heavy defeat the Germans suffered at Stalingrad, the Russians began to move slowly back west, but the Germans still had great force and the battles were bitter and desperate.

CHAPTER 18

Spring 1943

The freight train that was on the rails left to go north and all that remained were a few freight cars, while we were still in our tailoring workshop in the village. With the regiment gone, there was not much work for us. At the same time our commander, Kostenko, received his orders to leave and he told me that he was leaving a junior officer to wind things up. The junior officer who arrived in our workshop to see what we were doing did not wear a uniform and was not very talkative. He told me to report to him in the village; he would give me a letter that I was to deliver to a certain location. Next morning, when he gave me the letter, he told me that the location was about ten kilometres away and he gave me specific directions how to get there. The terrain I had to cross was desert-like and flat, just sand and more sand. No trees were visible, only "kashmish," the rough, six foot tall straw we had used formerly as a sort of firewood. After walking for about an hour – I had no watch to know exactly but it must have been mid-day

– I noticed in the distance a figure who seemed to be waving his arms frantically, but his screaming was too faint to make out. As I got closer, I saw that he was a soldier; he was yelling at me, "stop, stop. Are you crazy. Have you lost your will to live?" I still didn't understand what he meant and increased my pace.

Finally, I was able to make out what he was trying to tell me. "This is a minefield, you fool," he yelled, and gingerly picked his way sideways to reach me. I now got a full taste of what the Russian language has available for curses. "Is it really so terrible for you that you want to commit suicide?" he asked me. I explained my mission of delivering a letter to a certain location. He took my hand and carefully guided me out of the minefield; then he gave me directions how to reach my destination. Until today it is hard to believe, but there were no phones in this godforsaken place, nor could the officer find a horse. A bicycle would have been useless in this sandy terrain, so the officer had decided to use me to deliver the letter. When I delivered the letter to a middle-aged Russian in a small, four meter by four meter wooden booth, and I told him how I had come, he told me that I was a very lucky fellow, indeed. He gave me an altogether different route for returning to Linaynoe and I made it back before sundown.

In the meantime we were told that we would soon be moved

closer to the front so that we could again service the trains. Before we were moved from Lineynoe, two events happened which affected my future. A few days after my experience in the minefield, a swarthy lieutenant came into our workshop and introduced himself as the political commissar for the trains from this area. He turned to me. "Michael Abramovitch (my official name in Russian – Michael, son of Abraham), I want to talk to you in private." He arranged to meet me the next day to go for a walk, and we would talk. I was surprised and somewhat apprehensive, but then I realized that if they wanted to arrest you, they didn't invite you for a walk first.

Next day he came and we took a walk, almost a pleasant walk. He questioned me about my family, what they did for a living, and how I had made out in school. I answered everything truthfully, and in a moment of courage, asked him for his family name because to me he looked like a Georgian. "Goldberg," he answered without hesitation, and now I knew who I was dealing with. After questioning me about all my family details, he told me that he was convinced that I was a very responsible youth and he would like to propose me for membership in the "Komsomol," the communist youth organization that prepared young people for leadership roles in the communist regime. Now followed a lecture on how good it was to be in the leadership group and to build the happy society where we lived. I listened attentively to his monologue and thought carefully how to respond to his invitation. When he finished, I told him that I appreciated his offer, but I did not feel worthy yet to be accepted into the "Komsomol" and I hoped in time to be truly worthy of the honour. Thus ended our conversation; we parted in a friendly manner but I never saw him again.

Relationships with David Israelit, "Dudko," were not good. He was constantly threatening to remove the sewing machine. We never knew what his aim was; he was extremely greedy and also a liar. Now that there was little tailoring work and we were getting ready to leave Lineynoe, the headquarters decided to dissolve the tailoring workshop and assigned us again to work on the railway tracks. We had been three: Shaya Farbiash, David Israelit, and I. One day we were ordered to the railway lines to prepare the few freight cars that had remained for the approaching departure. Shaya, I, and a few others cleaned the cars, but "Dudko" was nowhere in sight. When we returned from work to our hut in the village, we found that the sewing machine had vanished as had "Dudko."

CHAPTER 19

Trying to Remain Hopeful

We had moved from our hut to the wagons we had cleaned and prepared for living in them by building primitive bunks along the sides. Within hours we joined the main freight train consisting of over forty such wagons all similarly occupied. Some of the wagons contained supplies and some were occupied by the officers. Altogether we must have been over 600 personnel. We were told by the wagon bosses that we were leaving this area and that our journey would take a month, with stops in certain places. After lengthy preparations we finally departed north, in the direction of besieged Stalingrad, the city whose destiny helped to determine the ultimate end of the war. The commander of our train turned out to be Kostenko and I was happy to meet him again.

At the first opportunity, when we were shunted aside and had stopped for a few hours to let other trains with military supplies pass us, I spoke with him and suggested that it would be good to organize a tailoring operation again. He agreed that it would be good and if we could find a sewing machine, it could be a stable operation.

About ten kilometres from Stalingrad our train stopped and we were told that we would be there for a few days. I went to Kostenko and proposed that Shaya and I should go into the city and see if we could purchase a sewing machine. The Colonel looked at me, astounded, and replied. "Michael Abramovitch, you are not thinking very clearly. It is only two months since the siege was lifted; the city is completely in ruins after the battles which raged in and around the city." But I persisted and told him that I had a feeling that we might still be surprised and be able to find what seemed impossible. Eventually he let himself be convinced and gave us a pass so that we would be able to get around legitimately. After a few hours walking north along the railway tracks we found ourselves on the outskirts of Stalingrad. We had been stopped a few times but Kostenko's pass did the job and we were allowed to continue. Already in the distance we were able to discern the ruins of factories and houses. Getting closer we noticed what seemed like an artificial mountain. Coming even closer we got an unbelievable picture that we had not expected. The mountain was made up of hundreds and hundreds of destroyed German army trucks, canons, armoured vehicles of all kinds and tanks, all of this in a massive jumble. In some of the vehicles and in between were visible the bloated bodies of German soldiers and officers. The smell emanating from the bodies in the immediate vicinity of this 'mountain" was unbearable and we understandably avoided coming any closer. In any case, we were focused on finding our sewing machines. Circling the wider periphery of this huge jumble of rusting and destroyed military junk, we noticed even to our surprise a rusty sewing machine underneath some accessible broken trucks. We crawled under and managed to extricate it. It was a "Singer"! Of course we couldn't turn anything on the machine; everything was locked from the rust. Logic suggested to us that if there was one machine, there might be more. And sure enough, we did find a second one that we could free from the debris. We couldn't see any tables, however. We had learned once more that a war needs everything.

We continued in to the city with our two rusty trophies. The streets were virtually empty, but whenever we saw someone, we asked if they knew about a mechanic who could fix our machines. Eventually we lucked out; an elderly man told us that before the siege he had known a mechanic who fixed all kinds of machines and he told us how to find him but he was not sure if he had returned to the city. My mother always used to say, if it's destined then it will happen. Indeed, we did find the mechanic – also an elderly man, the young all being in the army - in the basement of the ruined building the elderly man had described to us. We struck a bargain with the mechanic: he could have one of the machines if he could fix the other one for us. We left the two machines with the mechanic with the understanding that we would return in two days to get ours. Walking past the "mountain" again on our way back to our train, we still couldn't believe our luck that we had found these machines and a mechanic to fix one for us. Now we carefully looked again all around the debris and sure enough, our luck held out. We found a sewing machine table with the wheel and pedals intact. It was hard to extricate (the tables were about 36 inches in length), but after about an hour we accomplished this too. Now we had to lug it back to the train almost ten kilometres away, and with the wheel, pedals and sturdy, solid wood, it was quite heavy and awkward. Shaya was a small, skinny man, so the main burden fell on me. I carried it on my head and shoulders most of the way back.

What drove me was the certainty that this machine would save our lives because we would not have to do the back-breaking work on the rails and we could earn more than the meagre rations that led only to death. When we arrived at the front of the train a group of the officers noticed us, including Kostenko. They couldn't believe that we had actually accomplished this almost impossible task. We explained to Kostenko that this was only the sewing machine table and that we had to return in two days to get the actual sewing machine. He and the other officers were visibly pleased; they knew that now they would have tailors for themselves.

Heavy battles were occurring on all fronts. Everyone was hoping that the Americans would finally open a Second Front, but in the meantime, the Russians were carrying the heaviest burden of the War. The front had now moved to the gates of German-occupied Ukraine and our freight train had already crossed to the west side of the Volga. There were rumours that our whole work battalion had been assigned to the "Donetsky" Basin, the centre of heavy industry in the Ukraine, with coal mines, metal and steel fabrication, and with many train terminals and connections. Our travel had taken almost a month, and food was scarce, though Shaya and I still had leftovers from our reserves during the prosperous time in Lineynoe. At the train stations where we stopped, we were able to exchange things for some food products. But there wasn't much because the Germans had stripped everything valuable and they scorched the rest to the ground. It was a bitter time in Russia. In Kharkov, Ukraine, we stopped for a few days; our first stop was

the "Tolchok," the big flea market, to do some trading. There I saw
scenes that shocked me. Wounded and invalided Russian soldiers,
most drunk to the gills, were shouting and cursing the Jews whom
they accused of being responsible for the war which had cost them
their limbs, and other such libels. At the same time these wounded soldiers grabbed whatever pleased them without bothering to
trade or to pay. The Russian military police were afraid to interfere
knowing that these were desperate men afraid of nothing. The poi-
son of anti-Semitism was very visible in spite of the fact that the
official policy forbade it.

Our freight train continued west. All this time I had kept
in contact with my brother-in-law Srulce in Charabali where we
had been mobilized. From time to time I even had a letter from my
brother Shloime, always with a return field number, not an actual
address. But occasionally, in spite of the field number, I was able
to figure out his approximate locations from hints in his letter.
When our freight train had arrived in the "Donetsky" area, we
were told that we would be staying for a while. The officers didn't
know what we would be doing, but rumour had it that we would
have to work in the coal mines in the region. Finally, our train was
shunted to an unused rail spur near an important train terminus
with countless rail lines going in all directions. It was the centre

of the coal and metal working area, in a town called Debaltzewo. After a few days Shaya and I were told that we would be quartered in the town, probably the same was done with the shoemakers. I never found out what happened to the rest of the hundreds of men on the freight train. My friend and I, and our precious sewing machine, were quartered with an old couple. The work we were doing was exclusively for our officers and it was convenient for them to have us situated in a private residence. The occupants of the house we were assigned to were extremely poor. The husband was an alcoholic and was constantly busy making his own hooch in a very primitive way or sleeping off the results of his labour. He terrified his wife and she was happy to have boarders in the hope that in our presence he would behave himself. By trade he was a miner, a big husky fellow, but, he was now sick with a number of ailments and incapable of work.

CHAPTER 20

In a Trance

With a resigned pain in my heart I still blame myself why I left my parents and sisters behind; almost sixty years later, I still feel a shudder throughout my whole body as I recall my feverish state at the time. How can I communicate that moment when we left alone without our parents and sisters. Why didn't we insist more forcefully that they must come with us. I feel that they would have submitted and would have been saved. For many hours at a time during those years on the trains, I would descend into a deep silence without being able to utter a word and I would think: "Mother, mother, will I ever see you again?" Weeks passed since we settled in Debaltzewo and we were working for our officers and their families. We had begun to acclimatize ourselves to our situation. I was expecting a letter from Srulce in the hope of finding out where my brother might be. Some days later I received notice from the post office to come pick up a letter. When I received the letter I noticed immediately that it was not in my brother-in-law's handwriting on the envelope. Eagerly opening the letter I noted that it was written in Russian while Srulce always wrote in Yiddish. The letter was from Donia Kamenetsky, the daughter of the neighbours who lived near us in Charabali. She wrote me that more than a year ago she had written to Bogoruslan, where was located the central office of records of all refugees in Russia.

She had asked if they had in their records the names of Avram and Chane-Mindl Gruda, and they responded that they had in their archive the names Avram Eliezer and Chane-Mindl Gruda and their family. I stopped in my tracks, and read the letter again and again, the words jumping out at me from the letter. Was this a dream? Was this real? I was walking in circles while reading the letter over and over. In the letter there was even an address where they were living, somewhere in Central Asia near the border with Iran. When I returned to my quarters, I excitedly shared the surprising news with Shaya and later with my superiors, and I began to consider what I could do. When I finally settled down, I wrote a letter to my parents to the address Donia had found for me. I also wrote Srulce, and my brother Shloime in the army, about the news and then to Donia. It soon dawned on me that I could not do anything until I had an answer from my parents.

I had lately noticed that my commander, Kostenko, had become very friendly towards me. During one occasion he confided in me that we would be staying only a few months in Debaltzewo and that there were plans to move our whole company to permanent work quarters in Odessa, once the city was re-occupied. He introduced me to his family, his brothers-in-law and their wives, all in senior positions, with the understanding that I would also be sewing clothes for them. He expressed a special interest in the news about my parents. In the meantime the weeks dragged on as I waited impatiently for news from my parents. I had fortunately found some books, including Tolstoy's War and Peace, and this helped me to pass the time and to counteract my anxieties. In the meantime, I received a letter from my brother. Reading it I re-read one line which at first didn't seem to make sense. He told me that in a certain village, which he named, he had encountered our landsman Shloime, the son of Avram Eliezer. Suddenly I realized that he was telling me where he was located since censorship forbade him to reveal his location at the front. He told me that this landsman sends me regards and would be very pleased to see me. From earlier correspondence from him I knew that he was an adjutant to a general; even today I am amazed that I had the nerve to consider what I decided to do.

Looking at a map I realized that my brother was about 400

kilometres away, approximately eight hours by train if there was no interruption. In my loneliness, waiting to receive an answer from my parents, I experienced an intense desire to see my brother. The question now became how I could convince Kostenko, my commander, to let me go and even get him to acquire permission from headquarters for me to visit the front zone. It is an aspect of my character, not always necessarily advantageous, that once I desire something I am not easily dissuaded from pursuing it. With courage I told Kostenko that I was going to ask him, at the first opportunity, for something that, at first glance, he would consider outlandish. But I asked him to let me explain fully what I was requesting from him. I was in this way trying to prepare him for an unusual request. I explained to him that I had discovered where my brother was located. He was near Melitopol in the Crimean area at the Azov Sea (the Red Army having already arrived at the Dnieper), and as our plans would take us permanently to Odessa while my brother would be moving further and further west in pursuit of the retreating German armies, he would be further and further away and I would not have a chance to see him for a long time, even assuming that nothing happened to him. I also divulged to him how I had found out where my brother was and he found it amusing. I also told him how close we brothers were

and that the news of my parents being in Central Asia had intensi-
fied my desire to see him since we had been apart for more than
two years already. I admitted that my request was highly unusual,
but I added that if I couldn't see my brother I would not be able
to concentrate fully on my work. I thought this last was my stron-
gest argument as I knew that he needed me; a tailor with my skills
would not be easy to find. Kostenko, a colonel in rank, looked at
me incredulously, shook his head in disbelief, and said: "I have
seen many crazy people, but you are really a special case. Everyone I know is trying to get as far away from the front as possible
and you want to go to the front area?" I imagined that he worried
that once reunited I would decide to stay with my brother, but I reassured him that he needn't worry about my return since I hoped
that he would help me bring my parents and my sister and her
child to the Odessa area where I could better help them all. This
seemed to convince him although with a rueful smile he reminded
me how risky my trip would be.

Now he had to arrange for me a "komanderovka," a special military permit allowing me to move freely towards the front
which was a restricted zone. It is worth noting that although I had
no official rank, I wore a smart uniform, a military coat, and very
good boots, as well as an officer's cap with a five-pointed star that

– although it was from the railway brigade – looked much like the military star on regular officers' caps. All this in some way suggested authority, perhaps that of a commissar. Looking in the mirror, I looked more authoritative than an actual officer, perhaps precisely because I had no visible rank showing. This was verified for me when I came on the train to Melitopol; conversation among the other military passengers immediately ceased, and as I moved forward from the door a number of the soldiers and officers saluted me and one or two offered me their seats.

The train stopped before Melitopol and I had to find a military truck going to the village near the front where I knew my brother was stationed. Arriving at the village I noted that it was full of military personnel; in the letters my brother had sent me, he had mentioned the name of a peasant woman in the village. When I asked people, I was directed to a house with a fence around it which turned out to be the quarters of the commanding general in this area. Knowing that my brother was serving in the headquarters of a general, I surmised that I would find him here. With my heart thumping I stood at the gate and looked into the courtyard where I noted a number of soldiers standing at tables doing something; on opening the gate quietly and entering I saw what they were doing. They were scaling and cleaning large fish, and among them stood my brother completely engrossed in his task. One would have to be a greater writer than I to describe adequately this moment as I called, "Shloime, Shloime!" Astonished, my brother and the group turned to face me, each man holding a large scaling knife. My brother and I rushed at each other, laughing and crying simultaneously.

Once we had settled down, he took off his apron and left his knife at the table, encouraged by his comrades to go ahead and spend the time with his brother. Undoubtedly each of them appreciated my brother's good fortune in having someone from his family visiting him right at the front. We sat down on a bench in the yard and began exchanging stories of our experience during the two years we had not seen each other. I told my brother that as soon as I was in contact with our parents and sister I would try every way to bring them to me. By then I expected to be in our new quarters in Odessa and I hoped that they would join me there where I could help them. My brother, of course, was overjoyed to hear that I would be able to help them; he knew how difficult it was to survive behind the front. If you didn't have some support – especially if you were older, like our parents – your chances were very poor when everyone was starving. When we had to part we couldn't make any exact plans because in wartime you can't make plans even for the next day. Understandably, we were very reluctant to part, but I had to return as I had promised and now I also didn't want to risk the possibility of not being able to bring my parents to join me in Odessa. A few weeks after returning to my base I received the first letter from my father. With shaking hands I opened the letter and shortly began to cry as I read it. He wrote that our misfortune is great; my mother had passed away, as had my two sisters, Ruchl Gitel, the oldest, and Luba. My youngest sister, Esther, and Ruchl Gitel's four year old daughter, also called Luba, were the only ones surviving. Along with my father's letter there was a letter from Esther, explaining that my mother and two sister had perished from starvation and typhoid. For weeks I was despondent, inconsolable, but eventually I realized that I had to pull myself together on behalf of my surviving father, sister, and niece. As I mentioned, we were preparing to move the unit to the Odessa region. I had written the terrible news to my brother-in-law who had remained in Charabali, and now we were waiting for my father, sister, and niece to come from Azerbaijan, more than a thousand kilometres away, to join him in Charabali. Early in 1944 we finally began our move to the Odessa region.

A train, a "shalon" it was called, of forty freight wagons began the journey. We, the tailors, had received our own wagon, as we had been joined by a number of additional tailors under my supervision. The train began the trip around 10 a.m.; the weather was frosty but dry. It was cold, but I was snug in my quilted slacks and a heavy quilted jacket called a "kufaika" and a winter hat that had ear flaps for protection. Suddenly, less than an hour after we had started, the train stopped.

CHAPTER 21

A Tragic-Comedy

From the many adventures that I had during the War which have remained in my memory, the following is one of the most important although, as an experience seen objectively, it appears almost like a burlesque. However, the consequences, had they been different from what finally ensued, might have changed my life drastically forever and the lives of those precious to me. Sometimes what appear to be trivial happenings can have enormously tragic effects. When the "shalon"(the long freight train) stopped at what was a small station, still partly damaged from recent bombardments, we were on the third set of rails away from the wooden platform. There were a number of other trains waiting. A lot of people got off to stretch and so did I, standing curiously on the platform. Suddenly I saw my commander, Kostenko, and asked him how long we would be waiting. "At least two hours," he told me. Learning that, I decided to go over to a little shack adjoining the station which served as an outhouse to relieve myself; it was always a good idea to use any facilities available because there were none in the wagons.

Relaxed as I relieved myself, perhaps even daydreaming about the future as I had been told I had two hours, I suddenly heard a train whistle. When one is constantly near trains that are coming and going, one learns almost instinctively to distinguish the whistles they emit. Something about this whistle sounded familiar, and still sitting I opened the door a tiny bit and I saw that one of the "shalons" was beginning to leave. In a second I realized that it was "my" train and pulling my awkward pants on, hardly being able to close the belt, I rushed out to the rails behind "my" train and gave chase. Even as I ran, trying to pull up and fasten my pants, the train began to pick up speed. Now with my pants finally on I ran faster and faster and began to close in on the last wagon. I can barely describe the terror that was passing through my mind. My passport from the Defence Ministry, with a special designation that allowed me to avoid the regular army, all my money and possessions and the sewing machine that was the security to ensure my, and later my family's, survival were all in the wagon I occupied. Where did I get the superhuman energy to catch the train? Today it seems almost fiction but it was all too real then.

Finally, perhaps almost two kilometres later with my last

breath, my chest burning from the effort, I was able to grasp the little rail to the steps of the little platform in the rear of the wagon, pulled myself on to the steps, and fell exhausted on the little platform.

I had made it! But my troubles weren't over yet. There was no door at the rear of the wagon; the big sliding doors were always in the middle on each side. How was I going to reach my wagon? We could be going the whole night without stopping because a "shalon" didn't have to stop at a station if it had the way free; and there was no shelter on the rear platform of the last wagon. The afternoon was wearing on and I began to feel the bitter wind and cold more and more; I tried to keep warm by moving on the little platform. It was already late in the afternoon and the wintry sun was beginning to get ready to set in the west. Standing like this I noted that the train was beginning to enter a wide, wide curve and I realized that it was beginning to slow down to avoid getting off the rails. I decided, with a fearful heart, to jump off the wagon and to try to race ahead to the next wagons as it slowed down. Soon I was ahead two wagons and got back on; now it wasn't as cold between the wagons. After a while, at the next significant curve, I repeated the same manoeuvre and got ahead a number of additional wagons. Fortunately, my wagon was not close to the front of the train, and after two more similar manoeuvres I was suddenly alongside my own wagon. Luckily the side door was partly open and some of the tailors were on the floor looking at the passing scenery and the setting sun. Surprised, they lifted me by my outstretched hands onto the wagon. Running alongside a train is no simple matter. One false step and the story is over. I was twenty four and in excellent physical shape from the work of the last two years, but most of all, I was lucky. Had the door been closed I would not have been able to alert my comrades and would never have made it.

CHAPTER 22

Kotovsk

For a number of hours I lay exhausted on the floor of our wagon, until I regained enough strength to tell my story to my fellow passengers, especially my friend Shayia. The awareness that I would still have the possibility to rescue my father, sister, and niece filled me once more with courage.

Next morning we arrived in Kotovsk, a town of about fifty thousand people some sixty kilometres northeast of Odessa. After a few days on the train, my friend Shaya and I were quartered in a private house with an elderly lady. The rooms were very small, but very clean, and we opened our workshop there. The lady gave us the impression of being an intelligent woman, not common at all. Tall, with grey hair set back in a bun, she looked quite distinguished. Sometime later we learned that her husband had been arrested as an enemy of the regime. For this reason she was happy to have us because she was afraid to be uncooperative with the military authorities. After a few weeks we relaxed and became better acquainted; we were happy to have our workshop in her house. By this time my father, sister, and four year old Luba were already on their way from Stalinobad near the Iranian border to Charabali near the Volga. As well, my brother wrote me that there was a good possibility that he would be getting leave for a few days and he would come to visit me. This news gave me a tremendous lift and, indeed, about ten days later my brother arrived. These were days of joy and hope. My brother, as I have mentioned before, had a very beautiful voice and one day we spent a lovely evening singing Russian songs in the courtyard next to the house, joined by some of our enthusiastic neighbours. My brother confided that rumour had it that his unit would soon be moved.

I assured Shloime that as soon as father would arrive at our brother-in-law's in Charabali, I would make every effort to get the proper documents to bring them to me. Then it was time to part; we hoped to see each other again, but understandably we parted with heavy hearts. A few weeks after my brother's departure, I received a letter that my father, sister and Luba had arrived in Charabali.

CHAPTER 23

My Misfortune in Rostov

When we arrived in Kotovsk and once we were in our rooms, we immediately – as was the usual procedure – went to the nearest market to see what food could be purchased. We couldn't have imagined the abundance that greeted our eyes. There were all kinds of vegetables and fruit, chickens, and milk and cheese. This was a very rich agricultural area, but still I was surprised. I thought that perhaps the local farmers had hidden the food from the Germans while under occupation, but now recently freed, made it available to their fellow citizens. During my entire stay in Russia I never saw so much available food. This was and still is also a wine-growing region, and I was able to buy wine in a pail to bring home. However, this abundance didn't last very long; after five or six months, the regime managed to reduce the area to the same drab scramble for basic sustenance that reigned in the rest of the Soviet Union.

One can see how the system worked in the case of our own

unit. Kostenko had a responsibility to find quarters for his senior staff which included even a medical unit. Our train workers stayed in the cars, but he had to feed them and supply heating and material. There was a shortage of everything, so he used every opportunity he could to find and to supply his unit. He decided to use the same method he used successfully in Lineynoe. Russians loved attractive, well-fitting clothing, especially since the existing choices were of a very poor quality. When Kostenko had to deal with high civilian or military functionaries, he knew how to offer favours. He bragged that he had in his unit the best tailors in Russia (his words) and he offered that his tailors would create outfits for them and their wives. In this way he received assistance in whatever he required.

For me this was a blessing because I was also able to exploit this situation to improve my condition. I write this so as to explain how I was able to achieve certain things that no one else at my level was capable of. Kostenko was dependent on me and I used this to my own advantage.

Knowing that my father, sister, and Luba were already in Charabali, and aware how difficult it would be for them to travel more than a thousand kilometres to the Volga and then south almost to Odessa, I decided that I myself would go to Charabali to fetch them and bring them to Kotovsk.

I had to get the proper documents for travel. When Kostenko heard my request to travel back past Stalingrad, he was not too
pleased, but seeing how determined I was, he acquiesced to my request. I asked him to give me a document that indicated that I was
travelling with two other people as I anticipated that I would have
trouble getting documents for my father and sister in Charabali
(my brother-in-law had written me that he was keeping his daughter Luba with him). Knowing that food was extremely scarce in
the Stalingrad area, I purchased two "put" of kasha (a "put" was
16 kilograms) for my brother-in-law. I calculated that getting to
Charabali would take about eight days, so I asked for a leave of
three and a half weeks.

With anticipation I left for the east, looking forward to
seeing my father, sister, and niece , and my brother-in-law in a
few days. In my anticipation, it seemed to me that the train was
crawling along. On the third day, before reaching Rostov on the
Don, police (militia) came on the train to check documents. When
I showed them my release that Kostenko had arranged for me, the
officer looked at it and then demanded where the other two passengers listed on the document were. I tried to explain that the two
other passengers would be returning with me. This didn't satisfy

him; he asked what I was carrying in my luggage. I showed him the two sacks of millet. With a gesture he ordered, "Pashli (let's go), we are going to the police station." The police station was not far from the train station and we arrived with my two sacks of millet and a bag containing my personal things, including a full bottle of vodka and a package of tobacco. When we arrived at the police station, nobody was there, it was empty. I tought to myself, maybe now was the time to offer him something, but I could not decide. In the meantime, he demanded my passport. I opened it and showed him the page where there was a special stamp marked "Bron", which meant that I was mobilized and could not be taken into another service. He replied I should return in the evening and "we'll see then." I asked him to allow me to tell him about myself, the millet I was carrying with me, and the apparent error in my release. At the end I told him I had a full bottle of vodka with me and as I finished I took it out and put it on his desk. He repeated "come back in three hours." I left my millet and also put the tobacco on the table then walked out with my personal handbag.

Outside the police station I realized that this could end very badly. Without my papers I was in constant danger because the military police were frequently checking the papers of young men, searching for deserters and anyone who could be suspect. Once arrested, they would send you to a military post and then, after some short training, to a unit at the front. Then you were cannon fodder. The hours seemed to pass very slowly; I tried to stay near the train wagons but to be as inconspicuous as possible. Eventually, the three hours passed and I returned to the police station, hoping that the officer would still be alone. I knocked on the door and heard him say "come in." He was standing at his desk and I noticed that my documents were on his desk and the two bags of millet were on the floor next to the desk. He picked up my release and showed me what he had written over it in large letters;"Vosvratit Adin," meaning "must return alone." Then he gave me the document and my passport; the vodka and tobacco had vanished. He told me to take the millet with me; I lost no time in leaving, thanking him on the way out.

Outside on the street I was perplexed; what should I do next? I had not eaten all day from worry that my trip had turned into a fiasco. I stood there, with few people passing, but G-d works in mysterious ways. A middle-aged man stopped, looked at me sympathetically, and asked "what has happened to you?" I obviously looked in distress. I answered that if he had time I would tell him. He nodded. I told him my story and I noted that he believed me. Then he told me that if I wished, I was welcome to come with him to his home and sleep over. I hesitated a minute, wondering if I was putting myself in danger by accepting this invitation from a stranger in a strange city. Then I agreed seeing that I really had no choice, and I thanked him. He picked up one of the sacks of millet and we trudged off to his place, speaking little. As in a vague dream I remember going up to a second floor room in a house on a nondescript street. He offered me something to eat and I slept over on a sort of couch in this one room. Such is the kindness of strangers and Russians can often be very generous people, sometimes sharing their last piece of bread. In the morning I thanked the man, gave him the two sacks of millet though he had asked for nothing, and asked him to direct me to the nearest post office. At the post office I sent off a document which Kostenko had also arranged for me which gave my father and sister permission to come and join me. I also had money with me and wired them enough so that they could buy train tickets to reach Kotovsk. That same day I left Rostov, but without luggage. Four days later I was back in Kotovsk bedraggled and defeated, hoping that the document and the money I had sent from Rostov reached their destination and would bring my family to me.

214

CHAPTER 24

The Unexpected Attraction

At that time in the Soviet Union, all news was disseminated by the government through the radio and by the state controlled press, chiefly "Pravda(Truth)" and "Izvestia(News)." The joke was that in fact there was no truth in "Pravda," and no news in "Izvesta." Still, I tried to read both papers when I could, but I don't recall any mention of the fact that the Germans were murdering Jews in the territories they occupied. What was always stressed was that they were murdering Soviet citizens, so we had no idea what was happening to our families who had not escaped. I remember that once in Kotovsk I met a Jewish soldier of the Red Army on furlough and his unit was on the East side of the Vistula across from Warsaw and they could see the city burning. He heard that there had been a ghetto for Jews in Warsaw and the people were all killed. This was the only time that I heard that something terrible was happening to the Jews under German control. The great Russian Jewish writer Ilia Ehrenburg, who was very famous and wrote in the Soviet newspapers –his articles had a tremendous impact because he encouraged the Russian people (it was said that an article by him was worth a whole army division) – he also never mentioned that the Germans were murdering Jews, but only Soviet citizens. Even he was in fear of "the Father of the Nations." Our spiritual nourishment was Russian propaganda. When I had a little time I would find books of the Russian classic authors; that also was my spiritual nourishment.

After my return from my failed trip to my father there was an announcement that all inhabitants of Kotovsk and the surrounding villages must gather on a certain Sunday in a designated field to witness the meting out of justice to traitors of the Russian people.

When Shaya and I arrived at the designated field, there were already thousands of people gathered and we could see an erected gallows with five heavy, dangling knotted ropes in the middle of the crowd. The crowd was eerily quiet; they spoke, but very quietly, almost in whispers. Turning sideways, I noticed two young women and I recognized one as the daughter of our landlady; the other seemed a very close friend from the way they held hands. They were both visibly sad with the second girl, her head down, sobbing quietly. We nodded to each other, the landlady's daughter and I. Suddenly we heard the motor of an open truck approaching the gallows though the crowd. It stopped right under the ropes. In the open truck were five bearded men with their hands tied in the back and a cardboard sign on each man's back and front. On one man's sign was written: "for rape – death!" On the next man's sign we could read: "for betraying the Russian homeland – death!" The third sign read: "for collaborating with the German fascists– death!" And the fourth one read: "for a cur, a dog's death!" In spite of their beards, we could see that the men were not very old. On the same truck stood an army Major with a number of soldiers. He gave a short speech in which he said among other things that these traitors sold their souls to the devil and the Soviet State would re-venge the death of its Soviet citizens. When he finished, he himself placed the knotted ropes on each prisoner and then gave the driver a signal to drive away from the gallows. The truck moved about three meters and we saw the five men, their feet also tied, as their bodies jerked in the air a few feet above the ground. I was not joy-ful, but I can't say I felt any remorse after what we had been told that they were guilty of. Within minutes we could see that they were dead.

Now the Major, still on the truck, gave a fiery speech about the battle Soviet Russia was waging against fascism. Looking more closely at the Major I suddenly realized that he might be a Jew. As the crowd started dispersing, I recognized our landlady nearby. I asked her if she knew any of the executed men and she answered that she knew only one, as did her daughter. Then she told us that it was the father of the sobbing friend of her daughter. Now I understood why the other young woman was crying. Thinking about this dramatic episode, in later years it brought home to me how we never heard, and the world completely ignored, that Jews were being systematically killed by Germans in perhaps the same fashion.

My commander Kostenko soon shared some good news with me. They were going to build a little building to house the tailors, shoemakers, and barbers, and that we would get additional tailors because a lot of work was awaiting us. At the same time I already knew that my father and sister were to leave Charabali to reach me, but it was not certain when they would arrive in Katovsk. They would have to come on various trains and, during wartime, these didn't always run on schedule. I estimated that it would take them at least eight to ten days to arrive. As it was, it took them quite longer because they actually left later than I thought they would. In the meantime we moved into the little building built for us, and although it was primitive, we were happy to have our own workshop. We continued to live with our landlady. I hired two additional workers, one a furrier. One was called Leibl (I can't recall his family name) and the other Hershel Shichman; both were from Bukhovino. Our little building was flush with the train tracks and on the other side of those tracks was the bombed out station which was still being used daily by the passing trains which stopped there. I used to take a break daily and run across to the station to observe the arriving passengers.

One day, while I was walking on the station platform deep in thought, I suddenly felt someone embracing me and shrieking "Moishe, Moishe!" I turned around astonished. It was my youngest sister Esther, much changed, and she kept calling "Tate, Tate (Father, father), it is Moishe, Moishe" to my father who was sitting on a bundle on the platform. My father ran over to join us; I could hardly recognize him - he had changed so much. With tears in our eyes we embraced each other. He was then hardly fifty-five years old, but the two war years had taken their toll on him. For a number of minutes we stood like this on the railway platform, all three sobbing uncontrollably. This is what our vibrant, healthy family had been reduced to. I looked at my father in his torn coat, thin and undernourished, his cheeks hollow, his eyes almost dimmed. My sister was then only nineteen, also thin and undernourished.

She told me that they had already been waiting for a number of hours at the station and couldn't find out where we lived. It broke my heart to look at them.

Ten minutes later we were at our room; the landlady prepared warm water so that they could wash properly after such a long journey. Then, finally, they had a meal that they had not had since we had parted in June 1941. In a few days I found a much larger room for all of us; my immediate concern was to bring my father and sister back to normal health and well-being. I had to make new clothing for them for they had arrived virtually without anything and almost in rags. It took a few weeks, but what a change for the better (the two accompanying pictures tell the before and after story very vividly). Slowly, as my father healed, I heard the story of what happened to them after we left Sarny. Day after day, Jews kept leaving the town and my family joined them on the last train. They ended up deep in Russia, near Stalinobad; my mother and two older sister perished from hunger and typhoid. How deeply I regretted at not being able to convince them to join us when we left.

Soon my commander Kostenko brought me some very important clients, the chief military prosecutor for the whole area, and a certain Colonel Kutzeruba, the head of all the railway commands in the area. I understood that I had to satisfy them so that my boss would be satisfied. As a consequence, I soon received from Kutzeruba a horse-drawn wagon of coal, a precious fuel in winter. In the meantime I tailored clothing for them and their wives from materials that most of us wouldn't have seen in any store, even if there had been any.

Fierce battles were then raging in Poland between the Red Army and the retreating Germans. We knew by then that Germany would lose the War; when the Allies opened the Second Front in Normandy we had no doubt in victory and the total downfall of the Axis powers. The Germans were putting up desperate resistance and the battles were bitter and costly in lives. Within a short time it was obvious that my friend Shaya who worked with me as a tailor and my sister were attracted to each other and would soon want to marry. And, indeed, in less than a year from the date my father and sister had joined us, Shaya became part of our family. Of course, there was no question of an elaborate Jewish wedding. We gathered a few Jews as witnesses for the "Arrey-at," the Jewish sanctification blessing, and afterwards they registered themselves as a married couple at the local authorities.

CHAPTER 25

I, As a "Shtadlan"(Intercessor)

Kostenko informed me one day that the commander of the civil police for Kotovsk was coming to see me. He arrived the next day and informed me that Mrs. Roosevelt, the wife of the American President, had donated navy-blue wool gabardine for uniforms for the civil police in the entire Odessa district and that he had received enough for his unit of 35 men. He wanted me to undertake the job of tailoring the 35 uniforms. It would be a large undertaking but there were distinct advantages. Of course, I agreed with pleasure; not only would I likely be left with enough material for additional personal use, but getting on the good side of the police commander was also important. At the same time, I tailored a fur-trimmed woman's coat for the mistress of the chief prosecutor, a beautiful young woman, while earlier I had already made a coat for his wife. He asked me to be discrete and, of course, I wasn't going to cross him. Moreover, gossip was not part of my style.

One day, my co-worker Leibl came to work and told the following story. His landlady and her husband had recently returned from evacuation in Tashkent and her husband was now a senior administrator for the office of distribution of food supplies for the local population. The landlady had a brother in Moscow who had come to visit her in Kotovsk. In Moscow there was a great shortage of food while Kotovsk was in a better situation and it wasn't difficult to buy foodstuffs. Before leaving Moscow he bought up a lot of plastic clothespins, difficult to find in smaller cities like Kotovsk. While he was with his sister, he managed to sell his supplies of clothespins for a tidy profit, and purchased a variety of foodstuffs to take back to Moscow. When he arrived at the train station, he arranged for his three large suitcases with the food and three large cans of cooking oil to be placed in the freight car while he boarded the passenger train up front. As he was about to go in to his passenger car he looked back and noticed policemen removing his valises and the oil cans from the freight car. When he saw this he was in a quandary; what should he do? The train was about to leave. Should he go on to Moscow and leave his precious cargo behind? He realized that his name and address were on his suitcases and he would soon be inspected by the police in Moscow, a dangerous prospect for him. He decided to return to his sister and told her what had happened. Leibl continued; the landlady's husband, an important official himself, decided to go to the police chief and ask him to quash his likely arrest and the charges that would follow. The chief refused and now the family was desperate and they didn't know what to do. Naturally, her brother was staying with them. Leibl, aware of my connections to the Police Chief and other influential officers, suggested she should come and speak to me. I was a little surprised that he felt that I could do something in such a complicated matter. He added for effect, "it's like 'Tish-B'av' (the day commemorating the destruction of the Second Temple) in the house; they are in despair." He pleaded that I should meet his landlady.

I was a little naïve, but I thought of the dire consequences for a number of Jewish families if we couldn't quash the whole affair before it went further. As well, I was curious to see if I could have some influence with the police at a time when I was making their uniforms. I agreed to see his landlady and he ran off to tell her. Half an hour later she was at our door, in tears, but grateful that I would see her. She told me the whole story. When I saw her desperation, I took pity on her and I told her that I would exert all my influence to try to cancel this whole business. I myself, however, didn't realize in what danger I could find myself. I decided to go to the police commander at his office a couple of hours later. He greeted me cordially, but when I began to discuss the situation his face immediately darkened with anger. "What is this business," he shouted, "that everybody is coming to prevent me from arresting a Jew, a speculator. Just hours ago the fellow's brother-in-law was here asking that I drop the case. Let's be clear; I can't and I won't drop the case. If the brother-in-law had not come it might have been possible, but now everyone in the police station knows about it." He was very upset and I left him without having accomplished anything.

Now I knew that I had a serious challenge and that I would have to work strenuously to save this Jew. I decided to try my luck with the Chief Military Prosecutor. It was my one other possibility. The Chief Prosecutor's office was not far from our workshop. Later the same day I knocked on the door of his office. He received me very cordially and after exchanging some familiarities, he asked what brought me to his office. I told him that what I was about to tell him had nothing to do with my tailoring work, but it had to do with saving a man from a disaster, and that I had undertaken to accomplish this. Without his, the Prosecutor's, help it would be impossible. He became curious and I continued. I said I would tell exactly the whole truth of what had happened, which I did, and I also told him what the Police Chief had told me. After finishing, I asked, "is this a great crime, that this man had brought clothes pins from Moscow, where they are easily available, and when they are not available in Kotovsk, and when he was going back to Moscow he purchased foodstuff for his family? I imagine that someone informed on him and the police had to do their duty. But now, after the attempted intervention of his brother-in-law and the refusal of the Police Chief, it has become a whole affair."

The Prosecutor listened very carefully without interrupting, and then when I finished he said: "I see that you are very interested in helping this unfortunate man, and so I will help you. Tell the sister that she should tell her brother who is hiding with her, to voluntarily give himself up to the police. That's the first thing he must do. If he gives himself up today, I personally will go to the police station the day after tomorrow and I will release him." He even gave me the exact time that he would be at the police station. I had no choice but to do what he had told me, but I said that I now have a difficult task: to tell the sister to have him give himself up. I felt, however, that I could not ask for more and I went back to the workshop where I told Leibl to bring the landlady at once.

When she came and I told her what she had to do, she began sobbing again at the prospect of sending her brother to jail. I told her, however, that there was no other alternative as the police would find him anyhow, in which case the Prosecutor would not intercede. "It is the only thing to do; we have to rely on the promise of the Prosecutor."

A little later Leibl returned to tell me that the brother had given himself up to the police. I went over to the Prosecutor office again and informed him that the man had given himself up. I could hardly wait until the day after. When the time arrived when the Prosecutor had indicated that he would go to the police station, I left the workshop and stationed myself inconspicuously at a distance from his office. Sure enough, a few minutes before his scheduled arrival at the police station I saw his tall figure come out of his office and walk briskly to the station. I felt deep relief knowing that something good would come out of my effort. I waited for about 45 minutes until I saw the Prosecutor leave the police station and walk back to his office (all the offices and the police station were in close proximity to the railway station and not far from my workshop which was between the police station and the Prosecutor's office). An hour later I went to his office and he received me with a smile; he took out a file from his leather case and showed me the large "x" he had drawn across the file. Then he added, "now you can tell your lady acquaintance that her brother from Moscow is released and he will have his three valises and three cans of oil returned." Then he added jokingly, "after all, if there's no case, there is no evidence." And then he added again, "Michael Abramovitch, I did it for you."

Of course, I thanked him profusely and I was grateful that I succeeded in resolving the situation. For such matters, even smaller "illegalities," a prison was a certainty. It's hard to describe the emotions of the man from Moscow and his sister when they came to thank me. They wanted to shower me with gifts, but I refused and explained that I didn't get involved for any reward; I simply wanted to save a Jew from a severe sentence (which in those years could even have meant death from the hardships in the prisons). When I refused their gifts, he offered a tempting proposition; he had a beautiful nineteen year old daughter (he showed me her photograph) and proposed my meeting her. I was not yet ready for matchmaking and thanked him for his offer. I can't forget this episode to this day because I remember the initial desperation of the family and then their gratitude and relief. Under the communist regime, and especially during the exigencies of those war years, his transgression was a very serious matter, and his brother-in-law's attempt privately to influence the case made it even more serious.

In the meantime, our life went on. From our official work in the workshop we had not enough to survive because they paid us so little for a month's work that it wasn't enough to live on for even a week. My main income came from private commissions that I completed outside official working hours. Sewing even one women's coat got me 3,000 rubbles, enough to live well for a month. I was getting quite a few private orders; it's interesting that there were so many people well enough off to pay for such sewing jobs. These were mainly fashion coats for women. One evening, just after I had arrived home from the workshop, there was a knock at the door and I opened it to see a middle-aged man I had never seen before. He asked for me by name and I responded that it was I. He then told me that he had promised his wife a new coat and asked how much I would charge to do it. I answered that since he knew about me he must already know that I charge 3,000 rubbles. How long would it take, he asked? I told him that it would be a while because I had almost six months commissioned work ahead of him. He said he would bring his wife in a few days and then left. Two days later two men from the tax office appeared at my house and forced me to show them the work I was doing. Of course, they found all the additional commissions; I even had part of an almost completed coat on a mannequin. Some days later I received a letter from the tax department that I owed 20,000 rubbles. It was six months income. I realized that someone must have informed on

me. So, of course, I had no choice but to go again to my friend the

Chief Prosecutor. He agreed to help me but explained that I would

have to pay some penalty. He suggested 1,500 rubbles, something

I could certainly manage quite easily, but told me to wait until he

had had a chance to contact the tax office. And that's what hap-

pened; my friendship with this sympathetic man had paid off

again.

CHAPTER 26

The War Is Coming To An End

Late in 1944 we received a letter from my brother Shloime that he was already in Hungary. He wrote that there was a rumour that they would be sent somewhere distant. Six weeks later we received another letter from him that he was now in Mongolia.

An episode that I experienced around that time illustrates how the Soviet regime controlled its people. A young man of about 30, a genuine Russian, used to drop into our workshop and would gossip about various things. He claimed to be a correspondent for a newspaper and was reporting on aspects of life here. However, from his questions it was soon evident that he was researching much more than material for newspaper stories. Occasionally I would even walk with him in the evenings and would have to be careful what I told him. It was evident that he was an informer for the NKVD, the secret police. I had a Jewish neighbour who had returned from evacuation in Middle Asia, a photographer who seemed prosperous. He once confided to me that when he ordered a second suit or coat he always made certain that it was identical to the first so as not to arouse suspicion; this way people were kept unaware that he had a second suit or coat, thinking he was wearing the same one. This was one of the ingenious ways people would protect themselves from prying neighbours or informers, the inevitable accompaniment of a police state.

Early in 1945, when the battles were already on German soil, I was taking my usual stroll at the railway station during my break, when I noticed a long stopped train with hundreds of uniformed men, but not in Russian uniforms. The Russian military tried to keep people away from this train, but I managed to communicate for a few minutes in Yiddish with a Jewish soldier whose uniform insignia had Hebrew on it. He was from Palestine, in the Jewish brigade that was serving with the British, and he had been captured by the Germans. The Red army had liberated their prisoner-of-war camp and were now taking them to Odessa to ship them back to England through the Black Sea and the Mediterranean. Although we only conversed for a few short minutes, I learned some things about what was going on on the other side of the War. This was the only time that I met a foreigner in Russia. We were cut off from the rest of the world, but one has to remember that it was Russia that paid the greatest price in suffering and casualties in the war to destroy Hitler.

One needs to remember that with the successful advance of the Red Army on the eastern front there was also the beginning of a cooling towards Jews by the regime, which only two years earlier had sent leading Jewish figures from the Jewish Anti-Fascist Committee, like the great actor and theatre director Michoels, and the poet Itzic Pfefer, a colonel in the Russian Army, to North America to solicit war support for Russia. The Anti-Fascist Committee had worked diligently to help the Soviet war effort, but now Stalin began to pursue an anti-Semitic policy towards Russian Jewry that was planned to culminate in exile to Siberia, in conjunction with a hidden anti-western policy. His victories against the Germans seemed to convince him that he didn't need the Jews for favourable propaganda with the west.

The battles were still bitter as the Nazis became desperate in defeat, but we knew that the War was coming to an end. I often think of that period for which we had hoped so much. Yet we instinctively felt that something was missing; how would we fit into the Russian family of nations? There was a weight on our hearts. When War ended on May 8, 1945 and a parade was staged in Kotovsk to celebrate the victory, I should have been overjoyed, but instead I was rather sad for we already had a little more information about the terrible tragedy that had befallen our nation.

For Jews there was apprehension in the air for we heard disturbing rumours that the general in charge of all the railways in the Odessa region, a Jew by the name of Levine, had been dismissed from his position even though earlier he was constantly praised for his work. Other firings of senior Jewish personnel followed. We could feel the change in the regime's attitude to Jews. There was a systematic, if at first veiled, propaganda against the so-called "cosmopolitans," meaning of course Jews. It meant that the Jews were seen as disloyal to the fatherland because, after all, they didn't have their own homeland. This campaign gathered more strength later with the arrest, and eventual murder, of the Yiddish writers and then the alleged doctors' plot against Stalin. These doctors were described in the papers as "murderers in white gowns," and a period of open, state-sanctioned anti-Semitism began. We felt its beginnings immediately after the War.

In the early months of 1945, we read an announcement in the papers that Russia had made an agreement with the Polish Government in Exile in London that it would allow repatriation of Polish citizens to Poland. At the end of 1945 we decided to register that we wished to return to Poland.

At this time my material situation was quite good. I decided to inform my commander, Kostenko, that we planned to return to Poland. He saw that he would not be able to change my mind. Nevertheless, he said to me, "you may be better off materially in Poland, but liberty you will certainly lose there." According to his perception, nowhere was anyone freer than in Russia. Understandably, I didn't wish to debate this question with him. I only answered that we hoped to find our families who had stayed behind. Even then we still didn't fully know what had happened to the Jews under the Nazis; we only learned about it when we returned to Poland in 1946, a year after the War ended.

Curiously, a day before we left Russia there were elections for the Supreme Soviet. We didn't go to vote and an officer from the NKVD arrived and ordered us to do so; they had to have 100% participation. I had a lot of acquaintances in the railway management, so I received a whole empty wagon for use just by ourselves. We were able to take with us a lot of food and other things. The entire train was made up of freight wagons. I have to admit that I left Russia with mixed feelings: on the one hand I was grateful that they had sheltered us from the Germans, but on the other hand, I saw the "big lie" about "equality" that was supposed to be the guiding spirit of the regime and which they trumpeted over the world. In fact, however, this "equality" was one big bluff. I felt very close to the Russian people in comparison to the Poles of my birthplace and to the pre-war Polish government who had made Jewish life so difficult in Poland.

We left Russia without knowing where we would make our home. It was not easy to make the decision to return to Poland for we knew we would not be returning to Rozhan. It had been destroyed already at the beginning of the War in 1939. The War had come to an end but our mood was sombre. While travelling west for a few weeks and seeing the ruined towns and villages which the War had created our mood grew even darker. In Russia we had left our dead mother and two sisters somewhere in the east on the steppes of Tajikistan, with my brother Shloime somewhere in Manchuria or Mongolia, and not knowing anything about our oldest brother Itche (Yitzchak) and his wife and child, we left in a very sombre state. Only much later did we learn that my brother and his family had been murdered along with everyone in the mass shootings outside of Pinsk.

The trip took a long time with many stops. Often Jewish people who had already returned to Eastern Poland boarded our train, including our wagon. Finally we passed Lwow and then Przemysl, and when we reached Grzeshow, I decided to go out and explore a little while the train was stopped. As I reached the first street opposite the station, I noticed a sign over a shop window announcing "Krawietz," tailor in Polish. I went in and a middle-aged man greeted me with "what can I do for you?" I answered, "I don't need anything, but as I am also a tailor, a Polish citizen repatriated from Russia, I just came in to exchange a few words." He, in turn, responded with a question. "Oh, have a lot of Jews survived? You don't even speak a good Polish but with a Russian accent. You don't belong here." This was my first encounter on Polish soil; I felt as if someone had doused me with a pail of freezing water. I left quickly, feeling that there would be no room for us in Poland.

While continuing further west in our "shalon," we heard that we were travelling to the eastern areas of Germany that had been ceded to Poland in compensation for the territories of former eastern Poland seized by Russia for Belarus and the Ukraine, as agreed at the Yalta Conference. Finally we arrived in Richbach, a large German town ceded to Poland. Train officials told us that we must disembark here. We went into the train station and we were told that there was a Jewish Committee in town charged with helping Jewish people repatriated from Russia. When we found the Committee, we were told that we would have an apartment in a week. In the meantime they directed us to a "kibutz" that would house and feed us. These "kibbutzim" were supported by the Joint (the Joint Distribution Committee, a US charity which had been founded before W.W.I to aid Jewish refugees). We decided to go to the "kibutz," as we were convinced that with the aid of this "kibutz" we would be able to leave Poland.

In the few months that we spent in the "kibutz," we encountered various people, some of whom were survivors of the concentration camps in Poland and Germany. Now we found out the full horror that had overtaken the Jewish people in Europe during the War. The biggest impression that remained with me from the "kibutz" was the ghetto songs we sang in the evenings, songs composed in the ghettos which gave a picture of what Jews had experienced in that hell. These songs burned themselves into my memory even more than the actual descriptions.

A noted occasion was the visit to the "kibutz" of Itzhak "Antek" Zukerman, Mordechai Anilewich's second-in-command during the Warsaw Ghetto Uprising in April-May 1943.

CHAPTER 27

A Fortunate Meeting

In our kibutz we heard that a number of "shalons" were coming out of Russia to a neighbouring city, Shwidnitz, an hour by rail from Richbach. Something pulled me to go and meet these trains, perhaps a hope of finding a relative, though secretly I was hoping to meet girls who would appeal to me more than the ones at our "kibutz." I persuaded a like-minded friend from Rozhan, Srulek Chrobotek – still alive in Toronto - to accompany me. Since we had plenty of spare time, we took the train to Shwidnitz one day and happened to arrive just as such a train was pulling into the train station. And indeed, we met two families we knew from Rozhan who were disembarking from this train, which already made the trip worthwhile. We knew that this town also had a "kibutz" of "chalutzim" (Zionists wanting to go to Palestine), so we decided to visit and asked for directions. Walking along the broad sidewalk on the main street, we saw three young girls walking ahead of us with their arms entwined. They were obviously not German, and as we got closer we heard them conversing in Yiddish. I wanted very much to see their faces, especially the one in the middle whose figure and walk attracted me even from the back. Srulek and I decided to pass them to get a better look and I recall telling Srulek after I had seen the girl in the middle that "this girl I am going to marry. "It was half joke and half bravado, but I was smitten and so we slowed down to let them catch up and asked for directions to the "kibutz." They said they were from there and invited us to join them. Thus we began a conversation with them which eventually would lead to a "shiduch" (a match, mine).

At this time our greatest desire was to leave Poland, the cursed land responsible for so much of our suffering. Many Poles were also arriving to be settled in these formerly German territories now ceded to Poland. They had no love for us and expressed their disappointment that "so many" Jews had survived. Sometimes their expression included murder and we constantly heard of individual Jews caught on the trains and beaten to death or shot. A few months later the world was shocked at the Polish pogrom against Jews in Kielce, where over forty Jewish men, women, and children were brutally murdered by local Poles a year after the end of W.W.II.

I promised Mania, the girl in the middle, that I would see

her again when we reached the DP camps in occupied West Germany which Jews escaping Poland saw as a way-station to Palestine, America, and Australia. A few weeks later we were told at the "kibutz" that we should be ready to leave one morning, to be smuggled across Austria or Czechoslovakia into West Germany. This was all arranged by the "Bricha," the secret organization of the Jewish Agency in Palestine clandestinely moving Jews out of Poland and Central Europe to put pressure on the British to change their attitude to Jewish immigration into Palestine. The borders were not yet tight, so it was possible to bribe the border police to ignore people smuggling across.

When we had left Russia we had quite bit of baggage, but now we were told to take only our necessities since there would be some long stretches which we would have to cross on foot. Thus one early morning we were loaded onto open trucks which took us South to the Czech border. There were about forty of us. A kilometre before the border we disembarked and began our trek by foot. Every few hundred meters someone met us to direct us for the next few hundred meters. I had been asked to wait for the next truck to arrive in about 40 minutes and I joined this group to catch up to my father, sister and brother-in-law Shaya. This group in turn left someone to direct the refugees from the next group.

It was all very well organized. In this way we finally arrived at a small town on the other side of the border in Czechoslovakia. We were directed to the small train station and noticed that there were quite a few others already gathered there, most of them Jews. We also noticed that the outside station walls were full of written messages and we soon added our own. It was a way to communicate to possible family or friends who might come through this same station. We spent the night inside the train station and the following morning everyone boarded a train for Bratislava. We were met by trucks and were taken to a hotel called "Yelen", which we nicknamed Hotel "Nendzy," a Polish word designating poverty and misery. We stayed for two days, sleeping on bare boards in big halls. This was a transit station. From there we were taken by trucks to Vienna. We stayed for two nights in some sort of public building, perhaps a former school, in the American Zone of the City. The highlight for me was that some of us were taken to the Vienna State Opera, a magnificent building that had survived the War. I don't remember what I saw except that it was not a tragedy; probably it was an operetta like "The Merry Widow." For someone who had been only once before at an opera, in Odessa, this was an enchanted evening, hard to believe in the midst of our stateless smuggling across borders.

From Vienna they took us by truck to the American Zone in occupied Germany, to a former German military camp near Poking, now a Displaced Persons (DP) camp about 100 kilometres south of Munich near the Austrian border. Having left most of our possessions, we arrived with almost nothing. The DP Camp, also called the Poking Camp, was on a flat plain with rows of primitive wooden barracks. Each barrack was about 35 meters long by 12 meters wide, with rooms about 5 meters deep, a corridor of 2 meters separating the two sides of the barrack, with about 10 rooms on each side of the corridor. Each room had a small metal stove in the middle with a tin pipe leading outside through the wall for the smoke to escape. There was a small table and a makeshift bench. We slept on military canvas cots.

Our block, B7, was a Dror kibutz; other blocks represented other Zionist movements like Betar, Hashomer Hatzair, Mizrachi, and later even the Lubavitch Hassidim. A forest nearby provided wood for our stoves; we found a saw and hatchets and organized a block group to cut down a tree for firewood. At first we lived as a kibutz in our block, receiving dry foodstuffs and cooking and eating together in one of the rooms we designated as the common dining room.

Poking DP Camp was considered one of the largest DP

camps in the American Zone, housing refugees from Russia, partisans, and survivors from the German concentration camps. It was organized like a Jewish municipality, with all the ideological movements represented on the Camp Council which dealt with the day-to-day management of the community. Food distribution was the major concern, but there was also a small, makeshift hospital, with doctors, mostly Russians, an ORT school where tailoring and other trades were taught, and a school for children who were taught in Yiddish and Hebrew. As well, there were a number of congregations and "chedders" (orthodox schools), and a large hall for films, lectures, and artistic and musical presentations. There was also a small Jewish Police detachment. At its height, more than 6000 people lived in Poking DP Camp.

My brother Shloime was demobilized in late 1946 and with three friends he made it to Moscow from the far East. There he, too, found out that Polish citizens could be repatriated to Poland and left for Warsaw where he found out that all the Jewish refugees were congregating in the newly occupied Polish areas in West Poland seized from Germany. From Warsaw he, too, came to Richbach and found our messages that we had preceded him and where we expected to be next. Thus, late in 1946 he suddenly arrived in Pocking. One can imagine the joy that our little family experienced. Now my father, my sister and her husband, my brother Shloime and I were together again - diminished tragically, but at least together again.

Everything we did in the Camp had a temporary, ephemeral feeling about it because we all were hoping to escape this cursed land. There was much agitated talk that there would soon be a Jewish State in Eretz Yisroel, and in the meantime everyone hoped to be able to be smuggled to Palestine.

CHAPTER 28

Out Of Europe

At the end of 1946 I received the news that I had been eagerly waiting for. My girlfriend Mania and her mother and younger sister had arrived in Windsheim, occupied West Germany, not far from Regensburg. We connected quickly by mail and a few weeks later I travelled to Windsheim for a few days. She and her family were also part of a "kibutz" there. We were in love and every minute we spent together was magical, an incredible contrast to the horrors we had both just recently escaped. She seemed the most beautiful girl in the world to me and we happily planned a future together no matter where it would take us. We arranged for Mania to come to Poking to become a member of the "kibutz" I belonged to. Until then I had been occupied in the Poking tailoring workshop created by ORT, the Organization for Rehabilitation through Training. In the meantime my brother had found his own "bashert" (divinely intended) partner. They didn't wait too long and at the end of 1946 they were married. It was a time when young Jewish people were eager to re-establish families. This obviously was encouragement for us and on Tuesday, February 4th, 1947, Mania and I also became life-long partners. We had returned to Windsheim where Mania's mother and younger sister were still living for the brief ceremony and the meagre feast that Mania's girlfriends had prepared to celebrate our union. After a couple of days we returned to Poking to continue our life together and to wait for the opportunity that would allow us to leave Europe, especially Germany. We had hoped to attempt the illegal immigration to Palestine; it had become unbearable for us to be dependent on charity from UNNRA and the Joint Distribution Committee as we were in the DP camp. However, Mania was visibly pregnant with our first child and the Bricha wouldn't take us for fear of the risk.

At the end of 1947, an immigration committee from Canada arrived looking for tailors and furriers. Later, around the middle of 1948, we were asked to come to Amberg, not far from Pocking, for various tests and interviews. Finally, we were approved for emigration to Canada; it was a happy moment for us, but tinged with disappointment at not being able to go to Palestine and the fact that we had to leave my father and sister and her husband behind. We had hopes of being able to send them papers once we were in Canada. As it happened, however, my brother-in-law had gone illegally, of course, to Paris in the hope of getting good tailoring work. A month later, my sister joined him, but the attempt was futile; there was not much work in Paris and it paid little, so my sister and her husband returned to Poking. Eventually, a few months after I had become settled in Toronto I found out that there was a Member of Parliament named David Croll (later a senator) who might be able to help me. I went to see him, told my story in Yiddish, and got his agreement to see what he could do. He took down all the details and a half year later my father and sister and her husband were called to be interviewed.

The urge to leave was so powerful that we felt relief at the opportunity to leave. We still had to stay in Amberg for months until our final papers arrived and it was a hardship to be there, with as many as twenty people sharing one large room. Eventually we were taken to a transit camp near Bremen until our ship arrived. The ship was the "Marina Tiger," a small freighter, 13,000 tons, which had been remodelled to carry refugee immigrants to Canada. We boarded on November 19 and felt that we had finally severed all the ties to Europe, the continent that had given us such unbearable suffering and losses. We were leaving behind a destroyed civilization that had created a beautiful culture through the vehicle of its language, Yiddish.

The horns blew, the ropes, chains, and anchors were noisily pulled in, and slowly the ship, pulled by one tugboat, made its way down the estuary that led into the North Sea. As the estuary widened and the horizon sank further and further away, we could no longer see the shore on either side. Everybody went down to the lower decks and into their tiny cabins. Although some of the immigrant passengers had to share cabins, Mania and I were lucky to get our own, small as it was. For the first four or five days the trip was not bad; the sun shone and we were allowed on deck for short periods. The food was a problem, however, as it was almost completely strange to our palates. For instance, we were served white sliced bread which, to our East European tastes, looked and tasted like cotton. Of course, what little food we did ingest often found itself regurgitated as our stomachs rebelled against the heaving of the small ship. The last four days were a real horror. The weather turned ugly and a violent storm took over the area we were trying to manoeuvre through. At first the ship's staff forbade us from going on deck. They tied heavy ropes along the passages and along the walls of the dining room/social hall to make it possible to traverse the ship. But the heaving became so violent, the mountainous waves so high and threatening above the ship, that we began to fear for our lives. There was an incessant howling from the wind as it sent waves of brine across the upper deck. It seemed to us that the sailors who passed among us were just as worried; they too had seldom encountered such a violent sea. We needed fresh air; the vomiting left an acrid, sour smell throughout the ship that was almost unbearable. Finally, even the sailors realized that we needed relief and they didn't prevent us from going on deck, dangerous as it was. Mania and I did go up and found a less exposed area where the waves breaking over the ship couldn't reach us. We became drenched from the rain and incessant spray, but we decided that if we were to drown we would rather not be below deck. What little of the ship we could make out seemed like a little spool tossed around in an enormous, violent pool.

Finally, at the end of the third day the storm subsided as slowly and stealthily as it had caught us. We first noticed that the howling of the wind was ceasing and that the waves now broke on the ship's side rather than flowing across the deck. Eventually the rain stopped altogether and the ship steadied as she began approaching closer to the North American continent. The next days the ship moved steadily ahead only gently swaying a little from side to side occasionally. On the seventh day of our voyage the sun emerged gloriously behind us in the east and later in the morning we were told to pack and prepare to leave the next day because would soon see land. Of course, one of our chief problems was that we didn't understand English and couldn't always follow the instructions or news items announced over the pa system. A few people who knew something of the language tried to translate what little they understood into the Yiddish that was our means of communication.

The announcement aroused in us ambivalent emotions full of expectations, apprehension and hope: what did the future hold for us? The last night was largely sleepless as we prepared for the long desired moment of coming to America. When the morning finally came, everyone went on deck to witness the arrival. It was one of the most beautiful moments in our lives, when we saw in the horizon the first outlines of our new continent as it seemed to come ever closer to us. So this was the land! Slowly we could make out the contours of a city. Many of the Jewish refugees had tears in their eyes, both of joy but also of profound sadness for those in our families who had not survived the realization of this dream.

When the ship was finally secured at the pier, Pier 21, in Halifax, now a famous museum dedicated to the almost two million immigrants who arrived there to start life anew in Canada, officials from the customs and immigration departments along with local representatives of the Canadian Jewish Congress came on board to greet us. After some preliminaries, a representative of the Congress addressed the Jewish immigrants in a hard-to-understand Yiddish. Till now we had been herded everywhere like a flock of sheep, but now we were actually asked where in Canada we would like to go to. There was an attempt to lure us to St. John's, New Brunswick, I suppose to augment the small, though active Jewish Community there (Newfoundland had not yet joined the Dominion). A few accepted the invitation, but most of us wanted to go to the larger communities we had vaguely heard of. I asked to see a map and noticed that Toronto seemed quite close to Cleveland where Mania's uncle Moishe Manaster, her father's older brother who had left for America after W.W.I, lived. As well, Toronto didn't seem to be too far from New York where my mother's sister and two brothers had settled before W.W.I. So, we asked to be taken to Toronto.

All those who had expressed a desire to go to Toronto were gathered together and walked down the ramp from the ship to be processed in Pier 21's large hangar. After each was provided with appropriate immigration papers we were led to a bus that took us to the train station. It was a short ride. At the train station we were again kept together and someone led us to our train. We boarded an old passenger car with straw-weave benches, nothing plush, and after an hour's wait, heard the locomotive whistle and slowly begin moving out of the train station into the appropriate rail spur that led out of Halifax west to New Brunswick and then through Maine to Quebec.

Although it was late November and cool, there was no snow though the fields had a dun colour and the only green was that of the evergreens and the long stretches of pine forests we passed. The country was flat in places but with many stretches of gently rolling hills. Frequently we passed lonely, isolated farms, the livestock just then slowly making its way back to the barns. Often the train made a wide circle and we could see our black steam locomotive, about 12 cars ahead of us, leaving a dark-grey plume of slowly dissipating smoke, while at the other end of the train's half circle additional passenger and then freight cars followed us. It was a beautiful sunny day and well after lunch, yet we were too excited to think of food. For quite a while all we could do was look out of our window and marvel at the immensity and vastness of this beautiful land. Very occasionally we would pass on the outskirts of a village and once or twice the train tracks led right through the main street of a small town, something I had never seen in Europe. By 5 o'clock the evening had set in and a gentle

purple began replacing the bright day. Now we settled down finally to eat from the sandwich bags which had been prepared for
us by the Jewish community in Halifax. Water was available on the
train and there was a bathroom at the end of the wagon before the
exit platform that connected to the next car. Eventually the steady
rhythm of the click-clacking wheels lulled us to sleep; once I woke
when the train stopped for a few minutes at a small terminal, probably for water. Mania, now visibly pregnant with our son Michael,
was in a better mood ever since we had gotten off the ship. When
I awoke, she was still sleeping curled up on the rest of our bench,
her head slumped on the make-shift pillow, made up of an extra
jacket that she had worn under her coat, that she had carefully
folded to fit over the armrest next to the window. The coat now
served as her blanket.

When I woke, it must have been around six or seven in the
morning (my watch was not yet set for Canadian time, and we had
crossed at least one time zone, probably gaining an hour). I looked
out of the window trying carefully not to wake Mania and after a
little while I noticed that we were occasionally passing alongside
a body of water without seeing the other side. I assumed it was a
lake; only years after, by chance looking at a large map of Canada
I realized it must have been the St. Lawrence as it slowly narrows

towards Quebec City. A few hours later I was able to see the other shore whenever the train came closer to the water. Finally, after a number of hours, I could see in the distance the outlines of larger buildings and something that looked like a castle. It was, of course the citadel which was the fortified Old Town of Quebec City. Soon the train crossed to the other side on what to me seemed a very long bridge. About half an hour later we slowly pulled into a large station with quite a few railway spurs and a number of lengthy concrete or cement platforms. Our train now uncoupled some of the freight cars at the back while from one of the passenger cars forward emerged some twenty five or thirty immigrants, children included, who had chosen to come to Quebec. They may have been immigrants, not necessarily from our ship, who had come from France or Belgium and had chosen Quebec City because they spoke French.

After about an hour, probably with some new freight cars loaded with mail and products newly attached to our train, we began to move slowly out of the station and within about 20 minutes were again going at a steady pace towards Montreal. Now, much more frequently than earlier we could see the mighty St.Lawrence River to our left. We made one more significant stop, about twenty minutes, at Trois Rivieres and then continued at a steady clip to

Montreal. Almost exactly at 5pm we arrived in Windsor Station.

Representatives of the Montreal Jewish community and of JIAS (Jewish Immigrant Aid Society) were there to greet us as soon as we entered from the train platform into the main Windsor Station Hall. After some words of greeting in Yiddish, we were directed to waiting buses outside. One bus was for those who were staying in Montreal; the other one was for those going on the next day to Toronto and points west. As our bus driver drove past intersections, I remember being astounded that he stopped without seeing any policeman to direct him. We had not seen traffic lights in the cities we had been to in Poland and Germany. After about 20 minutes we stopped on a busy shopping street with a lot of sidewalk traffic where we were ushered into a sizable Restaurant called "Moishe's." Later we were to learn that this was St. Lawrence Street, the famed Main, and the restaurant was, even then, the fabled "Moishe's Steak House." I don't recall what we ate, probably steak, but I remember that a jovial man, the owner, still with an apron around his waist, circulated among us, clearly delighted to play host. I don't recall where they took us to sleep, perhaps it was in a hall in the Davis Building, the old YMHA on Mount Royal Street near the corner of Park Avenue, where they had prepared cots with sheets, pillows, and blankets. I imagine we were neither the first nor the last group that they brought here before moving them to Toronto and western Jewish communities like Winnipeg, Regina, and Vancouver. In the morning, after a short breakfast of buttered roll and coffee or tea, kids got a glass of milk, we boarded the same bus and were taken back to Windsor Station to board the train for Toronto. Half an hour later we were on our way to our final destination.

Around a few minutes after 5pm, we arrived at Toronto's Union station. Again there were representatives of JIAS and of the needle-trade unions that had secured permission for us to immigrate to Canada after so many years when Canada had refused entry to Jews. A bus took us all to the Labour Lyceum, on Baldwin and Spadina Avenue in the centre of Toronto's former garment manufacturing area, which was the headquarters for the needle trade. Again we were registered and a representative of the Canadian Jewish Congress explained that the Congress had prepared houses for families, but single people and couples would have to find their own living quarters. Mania and I received $25 and were urged to seek accommodation in the immediate area as it was largely Jewish.

After we began to orient ourselves a little, someone told us that there was a room to let a block away on Baldwin Street near the bakery. We walked over and rang the bell. An old lady came to the door and we told her in Yiddish that we had been told she had a room for rent. She nodded her head and invited us in. On the second floor she showed us a very shabby room with a double bed and a rickety table that looked like it was going to fall apart; two chairs stood at the side. We wanted to sleep in a bed again and I thought we were lucky to find a room, so we decided to take it. She asked for eight dollars for a week and I handed it over. We went back to the Labour Lyceum to bring the bit of luggage we had had with us. While there we noticed a man, about 40, who stopped everybody and talked to them in Yiddish. We were curious and when he approached us we were only too willing to speak to someone. His name was Platner and it turned out he was originally from Galicia, not far from my wife's birthplace. Soon the reason for his sociability emerged; he was an insurance agent and had found that new immigrants, insecure as they were, could be easy potential clients. Nevertheless, he was useful in explaining some important things about life in our new city. One bit of information turned out to be very fortunate. He mentioned that he knew a young rabbi, Rabbi Avraham Kelman from Beth Yehuda Synagogue, with whom we became very good friends and who was very helpful during this time of our acculturation to our new country.

In the Labour Lyceum there was a man at a desk, a union official, who directed new immigrants to available jobs. I approached him and he gave me a piece of paper with the name of a men's clothing factory and the address on Adelaide Street, only a few minutes from the Lyceum. We returned to our shabby room on Baldwin and it turned out to be worse than we had thought. It had rats, and when you left any part of a loaf of bread on the table, by the next morning it had provided the rats with a feast. In the night you could hear them squeek; Mania was frightened to get off the bed at night. We realized we would have to move, our pre-paid $8 dollars notwithstanding, and the next day, after I returned from my first job, Mania and I went looking for another room.

Now we saw that many houses had signs in the front windows advertising "To Let." We were puzzled because with our lack of English we thought they were advertising a toilet. Soon we were disabused of our error and noticed that there were many rooms to let; unfortunately, every time the landlords opened the door and saw Mania visibly pregnant, they suddenly decided that the room was already let or unavailable. Finally we were able to find a room with a family that didn't object, probably because the room they had available was on the third floor, without water or toilet, and only a little electric two burner plate. We had to descend to the middle floor to get to the toilet and to bring up water for cooking. The name of the people we rented from was Skuretzky and after we moved in the next day we told them that we had relatives in Cleveland and New Jersey.

Throughout all the years of the war I told myself not to forget the address of my aunt in New Jersey – Beka (Rivka) Silverstein, 26 Palisade Avenue, Newark (in fact, I had written it on the inside of the vest that I kept throughout those difficult years) - but she didn't live there anymore; Mania had no address for her uncle in Cleveland. Our landlord offered to find their addresses and a few days later he was able to give them to us. Of course, he also had to phone our relatives and to be our translator; our uncles and aunts had come to the US when they were very young and couldn't speak Yiddish. The conversation was not very satisfactory except for the sheer fact that I was speaking to my uncle and aunt and my cousins. We, and they, understood very little, but they did tell us through our translator that they would visit us very shortly. When our conversation finished I could hardly control my emotions. My body was shaking as if from a fever. It was difficult for me to believe that I had actually spoken to the closest relatives, other than my father, brother, and sister, who were still alive because they had left Europe many years before I was born. A day later the

Skoretskys found Mania's uncle's telephone number in Cleveland and we gave him a call. Mania had no trouble communicating with him as he spoke Yiddish. He too promised to visit us shortly.

I was then working in a men's' tailoring shop and earning 26 dollars a week and 2.50 dollars was deducted every week to pay for our train tickets from Halifax to Toronto. A little more than one dollar was also deducted for union dues and other charges. I was bringing home a little more than 22 dollars, ten of which went to pay for our attic room. We had to live on twelve dollars a week; it was hard.

The meeting with our American family, with us the "Greene" from another world, is worth describing in a separate volume. So many years have passed since that encounter that it seems now like a distant, misty dream, but it is pleasant to recall it now.

In spite of initial differences in culture and attitudes, deep family ties overcame those barriers and we became very close, sharing our mutual "simchas" and taking every opportunity to see each other and to strengthen the ties that bound us.

EPILOGUE

The visit of my family from New Jersey five weeks later, almost an impossible dream before the War, ironically was realized because of the terrible War. Among the visitors were my mother's brother Max Galant and his wife, their oldest daughter Florence with her new husband Abe, just a few years out of the U.S. Air force, and their younger son Lester. My mother's younger, now widowed, sister Beca Silverstein also came with them to see us. It is very difficult to express the emotions that ran through us at this first encounter. My aunt Beca still knew a little Yiddish which made it possible to communicate haltingly. When they arrived at the house where we lived on the third floor, we could not all fit in the room and there were not enough places to sit, so we descended to our landlord's parlour. There our relatives asked us all kinds of family questions to ascertain that we were indeed related till they were convinced; and no wonder, we looked so strange after the war and even the years before in poverty-stricken Poland had taken a toll. When I spoke with them, my feet were trembling; I could hardly control my emotions. They helped with some money and especially seeing Mania's condition, urged us to find better housing. We took their advice and slowly improved our living quarters. When our son Michael was born we were already ensconced in Palmerston Gardens, with a kitchen and a separate bedroom. Finally we were living like humans. At that time I was already working at a women's apparel factory, still a sweatshop, but at least I was making over forty to fifty dollars a week, a decided improvement. We kept our now close relationship to my family in New Jersey, and around this time Mania's uncle Moishe Manaster came to visit us also. We were now beginning to acclimatize ourselves to the new land and its ways. A second chapter in our lives had commenced and it would be worthwhile to record it, the failures and successes that are the normal course of life, but it is not possible. I want to conclude this story of that part of our life with an appreciation to all those who showed us friendship in our trials to become comfortable members in Toronto's Jewish community. I had survived my first twenty nine years, the stormiest period in my life. Of course I left out many occurrence since I didn't keep a diary, but I'm thankful that I was able to recall in detail those harrowing years. They are told without embellishments and as they occurred.

It would be appropriate to write about our life here, a country to which we came without means and without knowledge of the language but it would take another volume. A strong desire to rebuild our life and to make up for our lost years overcame these initial barriers and we reached a solid place in our adopted community. I want this book to be a legacy to my children and grandchildren as a reminder that G-d's greatest gift is never to lose hope. I end with a short poem which summarizes my view of my life.

I slept and dreamt

That life was joy

I awoke and saw

That life was duty

I acted and behold

Duty was joy

Rabindranath Tagore

THE REMINDER

Kol Nidre night, 1939,

As we stood to implore our L-rd,

Intoxicated with their victory

They thrust upon us their tyranny.

They drove us from our place of preyer;

Trampled our Holiness; left us desolate

As their forefathers in former times,

But now more murderous and profilgate.

In 1939 this terror was mere foreplay

To the horrors yet to come.

Vanished in smoke...millions of us;

Can Germans be called human again?

Do we, persecuted and downtrodden,

Appreciate the miracle the present is?

We have power to stop being oppressed;

The World now knows what "Jew" means.

So with our heads raised high

We praise and thank our L-rd;

Our life and soul we solemnly entrust

To eternity and to His Word.

(translated from Yiddish by Hy Bergel)

Morris Gruda

MEMBER OF SCABRINI GROUP

Québec, Canada
2006